Nonfiction: WHEN UFOS ATTACK of Hostile Alien Encounters, Cop Dembeck and Unknown Boundaries, Baltimore, Md. First E-Book Edition Nonfiction written by Chet Dembeck.

The cover and contents may not be reproduced in any form without written permission from Chet Dembeck & Unknown Boundaries (http://unknownboundaries.com).

## Contents

Forward.................................................................................5
Chapter 1 Death of a Hero ..............................................8
    The Timeline ................................................................11
    Actual Transcripts from Godman Tower.............................15
    Mantell's UFO Makes a Second Appearance .....................17
    Mantell's Chilling Last Words............................................19
Chapter 2 – Terror Comes to an Island .................................20
    Operação Prato or Operation Plate ...................................20
    Rumors Flying ................................................................22
    Similar Burns Occurred in Venezuela.................................28
    Conclusion on Colares Island ............................................30
    Nefarious Nocturnal Bloodsuckers ....................................33
Chapter 3 – Alien Mutilations ................................................34
    Alien Tool Found at Site of Animal Mutilation....................35
    Ranchers Scared..............................................................37
    FBI Documents: U.S. Attorney General Spooked by Cattle Mutilations......................................................................39

    Possible Government Cover Up? ........................................40

Chapter 4 – UFOs Challenging Planes and Troops ......................41

    1976 Case of UFOs disarming and shutting down Iranian F-4 Phantom jets ....................................................................41

    Excerpt from National Press Club News Conference .........42

    Permission for Evasive Acton ..............................................43

    Pan Am Airline Pilot Tells of Near Collision with UFO.........44

    Soldier Says That He Was Abducted by UFO that Delivers Strange Message ................................................................46

Chapter 5 – More Government Cover -ups ................................47

    Disinformation at Its Best ...................................................48

    UFOs Crashes Scenes Cordoned Off, Then Covered Up.....50

    Grim Starling Reality...........................................................52

    Is This Why NASA Rejected President Carter's Request for UFO Investigation?..............................................................54

    Government Investigators: 'Something Big' Happened at Roswell................................................................................55

    Early Admission by Navy Commander That UFOs Were Alien Spaceships .................................................................57

Chapter 6 – Even More Troubling Cases....................................58

    Final Analysis .....................................................................59

    UFO Blamed for Killing Farm Animals – Documented Case ............................................................................................60

    Mysterious Hovering Object...............................................60

    No Markings and Little Noise.............................................61

Reporter Describes Incredible Sighting of Cigar-Shaped UFO over Italy ............................................................................. 62
Eyewitness Account of Reporter ......................................... 63
Shag Harbor UFO Crash Is Canada's Roswell ..................... 64
Did A Flying Disc with Inhabitants Crash in The Mojave Desert? ................................................................................. 65
UFO over New Jersey Described As 'Flying Metal Loaf of Bread' ................................................................................... 67
Project Supervisor Claims UFOs Have Threatened U.S. Missile Defense .................................................................... 69
Children Describe Small Silky Aliens Exiting UFO .............. 74
Newspaper Account ............................................................ 76
A Nanosecond Vision of the Other ..................................... 77
Ghosts in an Historic Mansion ............................................ 78
Various scenarios ................................................................ 80
6-Step Strategy for Human Survival ................................... 81
Bonus Report – Ancient Astronaut Papers ................................ 82
Chapter 1 – The Discovery ......................................................... 83
Chapter 2 – The Watchers .......................................................... 87
Chapter 3 – Ancient Astronauts and Religions ......................... 93
Chapter 4 – Reasons for Denial .................................................. 99
Appendix – FBI Documents ...................................................... 103

# Forward

If there is one misguided theme I have heard repeated many times in and outside of the UFO community, it is the notion that UFOs and extraterrestrials are our benevolent technological and spiritual superiors, who are only trying to watch over us and gently guide human kind from a path of nuclear, biological and ecological self-destruction to an interstellar highway of spiritual enlightenment and prosperity.

This mantra has been repeated ad nauseum ever since the first UFO was sighted and close encounter was experienced. Yet, there is much documented evidence that these aliens, extraterrestrials or inter-dimensional interlopers may not always be benevolent.

On the contrary, there is much more proof that these uninvited guests, who boldly penetrate our airspace, have at times kidnapped, injured and killed innocent humans and animals. Thankfully, this wasn't the case in the latest, solidly documented close-encounter case recorded in a recently released Pentagon UFO videos. The usually mum Department of Defense almost appeared eager to report the Nov. 14, 2004 UFO incident, experienced by former Navy pilot David Fravor, who repeated a familiar story to all of us who have studied the history of Ufology for the last 70 years.

While flying a routine mission off an aircraft carrier he and other pilots spotted a UFO that made incredibly sharp turns and reached speeds impossible for an aircraft using Earth's known technology. As he watched this mystery craft zip away at an extremely high speed, he came to the same conclusion many of his fellow, military pilots have come to: "It was not of this world," Fravor told various news organizations. He added that no human could have possibly withstood the G force of such a tremendous thrust of sudden acceleration.

In this concise report, I will present to you documented evidence of a pilot unlike Fravor, who suffered harm in such a mysterious encounter. Such incidents are vastly under reported. For example, until I really started researching this subject, I never realized that a U.S. Army pilot became the first known casualty as a result of such UFO aggression. Although the Army denied this, and summarily covered up this horrifying event with no less than three different, ever- morphing cover stories, I will present you with documentation and eyewitness accounts from credible witnesses that prove within a reasonable doubt that on a January afternoon in 1948 hostile extraterrestrials committed an act of war against the United States. It was likely not the first – and certainly – will not be the last.

 I will also present evidence that proves that the population of a small island was terrorized, and its impoverished residents used as guinea pigs by an alleged flap of UFOs that harassed and injured scores of innocent men and women for a period of months. Some of these unfortunates still carry the scars from burns and wounds that were inflicted upon them by these unknown perpetrators. The proof consists of eyewitness accounts and secret documents that have been leaked out over several decades.

Additionally, in this report, I will document numerous cases of aggressive and hostile UFO acts taken against both military and commercial pilots. As a bonus, I have also included many little-known UFO sighting reports from the early 1860's to the present. Even though some of these are not directly hostile encounters, all of them invaded our airspace and in some cases, crash landed, exposing humans to potential injury or death.

Plus, I will present documentation of ongoing cattle mutilations that remain a dark mystery but point to either nefarious government and alien culprits -- or a collaboration of both.

In conclusion, I must warn you that some will not like this report. They will categorize my conclusions as alarmist and sensational. But as always, I leave it up to you the reader to decide.

After reading this report, two things will become certain: we are not alone, and the "others" have shown us in uncertain terms that they are not necessarily our friends.

**PS** - I've also included a Special Report on Ancient Aliens in this Edition.

Chet Dembeck

**About the Author Chet Dembeck**: Chet is an award-winning print journalist who has covered technology, government and the Pentagon for various news organizations in the Baltimore/Washington corridor for more than a decade. Chet has completed stints as a reporter for the *Washington Business Journal*, the *Federal Times* and the *Baltimore Daily Record.*

# Chapter 1 Death of a Hero

*Capt. Mantell'sF-51 Mustang was flung to the ground from 30,000 feet.*

On an overcast afternoon Jan. 7, 1948, 25-year-old Kentucky Air National Guard pilot Capt. Thomas F. Mantell Jr. became the first publicly documented causality of a hostile act of aggression by an extraterrestrial vehicle flying over Fort Knox, Ky., according to some UFO investigators.

In his pursuit of what he described as a "metallic object, and it is of tremendous size," the World-War II decorated pilot's F-51 Mustang was flung to the ground from 30,000 feet in such an unnatural way that at least one baffled crash investigator decades later made the following statement on record to UFO investigators Jerry Washington and Annie MacFie: "The damage pattern was not consistent with an aircraft of this type crashing into the ground," said James F. Duesler, a former Captain in the U.S. Army Air Corps.

Adding to the mystery and weirdness of the event was the fact that Mantell's body had been whisked away before investigators reached the crash scene. Nonetheless, Duesler and the other investigators were informed by a few equally puzzled officials at the site that "nowhere on [Mantell's] the body had the skin been punctured or penetrated, yet all the bones had been crushed and pulverized." Also, there was no trace of blood in the cockpit.

Despite all of these anomalies, eyewitness accounts and evidence that something incredible had occurred – no less than an act of war against the United States by an alien civilization – the initial statement from the Army about this tragedy was that combat-hardened pilot Mantell had lost control of his fighter as a result of climbing too high without an oxygen mask.

Furthermore, the Army asserted that Mantell had been mistaken in his visual descriptions of a large metallic object and in fact had been chasing the planet Venus, which it asserted had been visible on this hazy January day. After this obvious cover story was quickly debunked by astronomers, the Air Force, which had just been created days after the Mantell incident, stepped in with a second as unlikely explanation claiming that Mantell had perished chasing a weather balloon, which no one could document had been launched that day. When this explanation was also summarily disproven, the Air Force's final gambit was to claim that Mantell had in fact been chasing a top secret "Sky Hook" balloon, but because it was top secret he and other eyewitnesses mistook it for a UFO -- case closed.

**Not Quite**

While it is true that skyhook balloons, which were first launched in 1948, were cone shaped and rose to altitudes of 100,000 feet, Mantell's description and one of the official accounts of the UFO or UFOs observed by tower operators at Clinton County Air Base on Jan. 8 1948 told a different story.

"A sky phenomenon, described by observers at the Clinton County Air based as having the appearance of a flaming red cone trailing a gaseous green mist, appeared in the southwest skies of Wilmington last night between 7:20 and 7:55 p.m. "

Plus, we are asked to believe that Mantell, an experienced and decorated World War II glider and transportation pilot, was careless and green enough to risk his life pursing an unusually bright planet or some new type of weather balloon. In addition, my research has turned up some evidence that Mantell may have had an oxygen mask that day, and as the only pilot in his formation that did, was chosen to pursue the UFO.

One of America's foremost UFO investigators Leonard H. Stringfield, who died in 1994, thoroughly investigated the Mantell case. He came up with the following tidbit that some postulate supports this theory.

"My informant, preferring anonymity, related that he had talked with Mantell's wing man, who witnessed the incident. The pilot stated that Mantell pursued the UFO because he was the only pilot with an adequate oxygen mask. The pilot also related that he saw a burst of 'what appeared to be tracer' fired from the UFO, which hit the P-51 and caused it to disintegrate in the air!"

Research done in 1966 by Ufologist Coral Lorenzen added even more mystery and possible evidence of a government cover-up surrounding the Mantell case.

"The latest to reach me was from a captain in the USAF Reserve who claims he took part in the investigation of that incident, including the location and inspection of the crashed F-51. He supports the old theory that the 'spaceship' removed Mantell from his ship and then allowed it to crash. The captain says Mantell's body was never found."

While this is not definitive evidence that Mantell's body was indeed not recovered, it would explain why crash investigators never saw his body, or it being removed from the scene. But since it is not corroborated and because no one in the Mantell family every publicly said their loved one's body was not returned. The chances of this theory ever being proven are remote.

## The Timeline

But before we go any further into this mystery, I think we should go through the exact timeline of the UFO sighting and Mantell's untimely demise.

One of the best sources for the timeline of the Mantell incident is the investigative work of the late Edward J. Ruppelt, the first head of the Air Force's "Project Blue Book," which was charged with quelling the mass hysteria sparked by a wave of UFO sightings in the 1950s by objectively investigating such events. As such, Ruppelt had access to a great deal of the information available – some of which was being withheld from the public. Here are some of the facts Ruppelt gathered"

**Ruppelt's Account**

"At 1:15 p.m. on that afternoon the control tower operators at Godman AFB, outside Louisville, Kentucky, received a telephone call from the Kentucky State Highway Patrol. The patrol wanted to know if Godman Tower knew anything about any unusual aircraft in the vicinity. Several people from Maysville, Kentucky, a small town 80 miles east of Louisville, had reported seeing a strange aircraft. Godman knew that they had nothing in the vicinity, so they called Flight Service at Wright-Patterson AFB. In a few minutes Flight Service called back.

Their air traffic control board showed no flights in the area. About twenty minutes later the state police called again. This time people from the towns of Owensboro and Irvington, Kentucky, west of Louisville, were reporting a strange craft. The report from these two towns was a little more complete. The town's people had described the object to the state police as being "circular, about 250 to 300 feet in diameter," and moving westward at a "pretty good clip." Godman Tower checked Flight Service again. Still nothing. All this time the tower operators had been looking for the reported object. They theorized that since the UFO had had to pass north of Godman to get from Maysville to Owensboro it might come back.

At 1:45 p.m. they saw it, or something like it. Later, in his official report, the assistant tower operator said that he had seen the object for several minutes before he called his chief's attention to it. He said that he had been reluctant to 'make a flying saucer report.' As soon as the two men in the tower had assured themselves that the UFO, they saw was not an airplane or a weather balloon, they called Flight Operations.

They wanted the operations officer to see the UFO. Before long, word of the sighting had gotten around to key personnel on the base, and several officers, besides the base operations officer and the base intelligence officer, were in the tower. All of them looked at the UFO through the tower's 6 x 50 binoculars and decided they couldn't identify it. About this time Colonel Hix, the base commander, arrived. He looked and he was baffled. At 2:30 p.m., they reported, they were discussing what should be done when four F-51's came into view, approaching the base from the south.

The tower called the flight leader, Capt. Mantell, and asked him to look at the object and try to identify it. One F-51 in the flight was running low on fuel, so he asked permission to go on to his base. Mantell took his two remaining wing men, made a turn, and started after the UFO. The people in Godman Tower were directing him as none of the pilots could see the object at this time. They gave Mantell an initial heading toward the south and the flight was last seen heading in the general direction of the UFO.

By the time the F-51's had climbed to 10,000 feet, the two wing men later reported, Mantell had pulled out ahead of them and they could just barely see him. At 2:45 p.m. Mantell called the tower and said, "I see something above and ahead of me and I'm still climbing." All the people in the tower heard Mantell say this and they heard one of the wing men call back and ask, "What the hell are we looking for?" The tower immediately called Mantell and asked him for a description of what he saw. Odd as it may seem, no one can remember exactly what he answered. Saucer historians have credited him with saying, "I've sighted the thing. It looks metallic and it's tremendous in size.... Now it's starting to climb." Then in a few seconds he is supposed to have called and said, "It's above me and I'm gaining on it. I'm going to 20,000 feet." Everyone in the tower agreed on this one last bit of the transmission, "I'm going to 20,000 feet," but didn't agree on the first part, about the UFO's being metallic and tremendous.

The two wing men were now at 15,000 feet and trying frantically to call Mantell. He had climbed far above them by this time and was out of sight. Since none of them had any oxygen they were worried about Mantell. Their calls were not answered. Mantell never talked to anyone again. The two wing men leveled off at 15,000 feet, made another fruitless effort to call Mantell, and started to come back down. As they passed Godman Tower on their way to their base, one of them said something to the effect that all he had seen was a reflection on his canopy.

When they landed at their base, Standiford Field, just north of Godman, one pilot had his F-51 refueled and serviced with oxygen and took off to search the area again. He didn't see anything.

At 3:50 p.m. the tower lost sight of the UFO. A few minutes later, they got word that Mantell had crashed and was dead.

Several hours later, at 7:20 P.M., airfield towers all over the Midwest sent in frantic reports of another UFO. In all about a dozen airfield towers reported the UFO as being low on the southwestern horizon and disappearing after about twenty minutes. The writers of saucer lore say this UFO was what Mantell was chasing when he died; the Air Force says this UFO was Venus.

The people on Project Sign, a government program charged with investigating UFOs at the time, worked fast on the Mantell incident. Contemplating a flood of queries from the press as soon as they heard about the crash, they realized that they had to get a quick answer. Venus had been the target of a chase by an Air Force F-51 several weeks before and there were similarities between this sighting and the Mantell Incident. So almost before the rescue crews had reached the crash, the word "Venus" went out. This satisfied the newspaper editors, and so it stood for about a year; Mantell had unfortunately been killed trying to reach the planet Venus.

To the press, the nonchalant, offhand manner with which the sighting was written off by the Air Force public relations officer showed great confidence in the conclusion blaming Venus. But behind the barbed-wire fence that encircled Air Technical Intelligence Center (ATIC) the nonchalant attitude didn't exist among the intelligence analysts.

## Actual Transcripts from Godman Tower

While Ruppelt's account downplays Mantell's description of the UFO, the actual transcript of the conversations between Godman tower and the pilots confirm previous reports.

Here it is:

"Godman Tower Calling the flight of 4 ships northbound over Godman Field. Do you read? Over.

[Pause] Godman Tower Calling the flight of 4 ships northbound over Godman Field. Do you read? Over."

"Roger, Godman Tower. This is National Guard 869, Flight Leader of the formation. Over."

"National Guard 869 from Godman Tower. We have an object out south of Godman here that we are unable to identify, and we would like to know if you have gas enough; and if so, could you take a look for us if you will."

"Roger, I have the gas and I will take a look for you if you give me the correct heading.

One of his three companions in flight received permission to continue his pre-assigned flight plan, while Mantell and the remaining two planes headed to the coordinates of the visual sightings.

Mantell led the way in the climb to 15,000 feet, and upon reaching the position, he radioed the following statement back to the control tower.

"The object is directly ahead of and above me now, moving at about half my speed... It appears to be a metallic object or possibly reflection of Sun from a metallic object, and it is of tremendous size... I'm still climbing... I'm trying to close in for a better look."

### Why Did Mantell Risk His Life?

As I mentioned earlier, there was at least one witness to the event that said Mantell was the only pilot that had oxygen and that is why he was chosen to pursue the UFO. However, the consensus is that Mantell in fact did not have oxygen, therefore, this begs the question: why would any combat-hardened pilot take such a foolish chance pursing an object in such thin air?

One possible answer appears in Ruppelt's report:

"In high altitude indoctrination during World War II, I made several trips up to 30,000 feet in a pressure chamber. To demonstrate anoxia, we would leave our oxygen masks off until we became dizzy. A few of the hardier souls could get to 15,000 feet, but nobody ever got over 17,000.," the report said.

Possibly Mantell thought he could climb up to 20,000 in a hurry and get back down before he got anoxia and blacked out, but this would be a foolish chance. This point was covered in the sighting report. A long-time friend of Mantell's went on record as saying that he'd flown with him several years and knew him personally. He couldn't conceive of Mantell's even thinking about disregarding his lack of oxygen. Mantell was one of the most cautious pilots he knew. 'The only thing I can think,' he commented, 'was that he was after something that he believed to be more important than his life or his family.'"

## Mantell's UFO Makes a Second Appearance

In the beginning of this account, we mentioned the initial testimony of James F. Duesler, a former Captain in the U.S. Army Air Corps, who was one of the crash site investigators of the Mantell event.

The elderly man shed more light on the UFO, the Air Force's first claimed to be the planet Venus and later transformed into a top-secret balloon. In an interview with UFO investigator Tony Dodd, about the second appearance of the UFO early the next morning just before he was called by the Army to join a team of crash investigators at Mantell's crash site.

Here's his account, according to Dodd:

"Duesler was unaware of any further developments until 1:00 AM when he was awakened to return to the tower. A glowing, orange, cigar-shaped UFO was being observed as it circled in the distance. Reports of a similarly described object were coming in from St. Louis and Wright-Patterson Air Base in Ohio.

Duesler eventually went back to bed, but he would not rest for long. At 3:00 AM he was summoned to investigate a plane crash. When he and two other accident investigators arrived on the scene, 130 miles away, near Franklin, they were puzzled by what they found.

Because of the weight of the engine, he maintained, the Mustang should have nose-dived straight into the ground; however, it appeared to have 'belly-flopped' into a small clearing, doing no damage to the surrounding woods.

Although the wings and tail had broken off, the fuselage sustained little damage, and no blood was evident in the cockpit. The pilot's body had already been taken away, but Duesler was informed by others at the scene that 'nowhere on the body had the skin been punctured or penetrated, yet all the bones had been crushed and pulverized.'

Duesler admitted he found the circumstances of the accident strange. 'The damage pattern was not consistent with an aircraft of this type crashing into the ground,' he was quoted as saying. 'The official report said that Mantell had blacked out due to lack of oxygen. This may well have been the case, but the aircraft came down in a strange way.'

There is no doubt in my mind that the Air Force's version of what happened to Mantell was a cover story created to hide the nefarious truth that creatures from the unknown are invading our air space and there is little or nothing we can do about it. The fact that Mantell was summarily rebuffed by the visitors, who swatted his plane as though it were a fly, leaves no other conclusion to me than they are indeed hostile and not the benevolent creatures that only have our best interest at heart.

## Mantell's Chilling Last Words

*"My God, I see people in this thing,"*
*Mantell said.*

The most eerie and convincing fact that that what Mantell saw that afternoon in January of 1948 was something extraordinary were his last words.

They come from Richard T. Miller, who claims he was in the Operations Room of Scott Air Force Base in Belleville, Illinois. He came forward and testified before state and federal authorities that on the date of the crash he had been monitoring the radio talk between Mantell and Godman tower and heard Mantell's last statement very clearly.

"My God, I see people in this thing!"

Miller also said that on the morning after the crash, investigators had stated in a briefing that Mantell had died "pursuing an intelligently controlled unidentified flying object."

But within hours Air Force intelligence clamped down tight on the Mantell incident.

"That evening, Air Technical Intelligence Center officers from Wright-Patterson AFB arrived and ordered all personnel to turn over any materials relating to the crash. Then, after we had turned it over to them, they said they had already completed the investigation," Miller testified.

"I was no longer a skeptic. I had been up to that time. Now I wondered why the government had gone to all the trouble of covering it up, to keep it away from the press and the public."

## Chapter 2 – Terror Comes to an Island

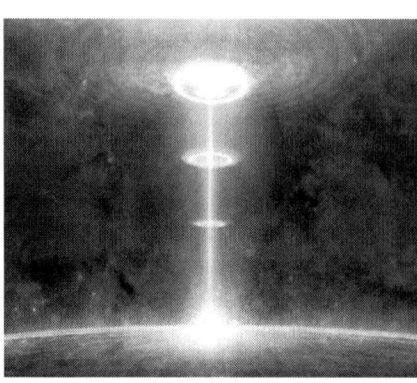

### Operação Prato or Operation Plate

In 1977, the 2,000 residents of the small Brazilian island of Colares were terrorized by an unprecedented invasion of alleged

UFOs that lasted a period of months.

After reading the documented eyewitness accounts of the numerous residents of the island who suffered burns, blood loss, paralysis or small wounds they claim were inflicted by light beams emanating from these UFOs, there can be little doubt that whomever or whatever was operating the UFOs are indeed hostile to humankind.

According to the government documents that have been leaked so far, none of the victims died, but many were burned and suffered other strange maladies.
Many told of having their blood sucked or removed from them by invisible syringes. Many of the residents called this the work of the "Chup-Chupas," which is derived from the Brazilian verb *chupar*, meaning "to suck. They used this term because they believed blood of "chupada" was being sucked by the beams of light UFOs aimed at them like lasers.

After panic nearly swept the island, the Brazilian government finally decided to act and conducted an extensive investigation of the hostile UFOs from October 1977 until January 1978 using intelligent agents stationed at it Belém Air Force base in Northern Brazil. During this period, the intelligence team carefully interviewed hundreds of witnesses in Colares and residents who lived in 30 other villages North of Belem. Many of these individuals empathically claimed to have been badly burned by light beams shot from legions of UFOs that invaded the area.

During this intense investigation, agents took hundreds of photos and several hours of film. According to prominent Brazilian ufologists, the films captured chilling scenes of the UFOs regularly diving into and coming out of water in the nearby Marajó Bay.

## Rumors Flying

While bits and pieces of information about the historic UFO invasion of Colares came out through residents of the island's mainland relatives, the government kept mum about the strange and dangerous goings on.
It took a yearlong campaign by the Brazilian UFO magazine *Revista UFO,* gathering 36,000 signatures demanding that the records of this investigation be made public, before Brazilian Air Force leaders agreed to meet with a group of Brazilian ufologists on May 20. 2005.

During this meeting six ufologists could review some of the classified files from the Air Force's archives, including those of Operação Prato, which means "Operation Plate, or saucer" in Portuguese. This included 110 photographs and 160 documents from the investigation.

Photocopies of many of these documents have been leaked to the public, including 18 photographs. The documents include the summaries of more than 300 sightings that occurred in Colares and surrounding villages during the UFO swarm.

What makes these sightings so credible is that fact that half of the sightings were witnessed by the head of the investigation Captain Uyrangê Hollanda or his six sergeants.

After he retired as a lieutenant colonel Hollanda granted an interview to ufologists Bob Pratt and Cynthia Luce.

"He told us "many people" had been burned by UFOs during the UFO wave, both on the Colares Island side of Marajó Bay and on Marajó Island," Pratt said. "Of the dozens of documents that were leaked, only a few mentioned any burns or injuries, and there is no mention of anyone dying."

According to Pratt, a former newspaper reporter who passed away in 2005, the investigation team photographed burn victims, although how many is not known. "A doctor once told Belém researcher Daniel Rebisso Giese that a colonel had shown him many photos of people who had been burned. And in 1993, Pratt and Gliese interviewed one victim, Manoel Emídio Campo de Oliveira, who said investigators took photographs of a burn on the top of his left thigh. Geisel, a biologist, has done more research on the Colares flap than anyone else and has published a book about it, *Vampiros Extraterrestres na Amazônia,"* Pratt wrote in a report for the Mutual UFO Network (MUFON).

Here are some of the most interesting eyewitness accounts from victims of UFO attacks on the island, according to copied government documents provided and translated by Pratt, courtesy of MUFON:

**On Oct. 11, 1977 at 3:30 a.m.** at Santo Antônio do Ubintuba - Rio Bituba, side road at Km 32, PA-16.

Miguel Arcângelo Soares, 32, literate, farm worker. He lives in the locality known as Vila Nova do Ubintuba and was getting ready to go to the village of Vigia when he heard his neighbors shouting "There it goes! There it goes!"

He left his house using the back door in time to see a reddish-yellow light moving slowly about 60 meters high, going SE/NW (Santo Antônio do Ubintuba), emitting a ray of blue light; frightened, he yelled to his wife to stay in the house... he went back inside the house and felt as if he had had an electric shock from a ray of light... like a charge of static electricity... He felt partially paralyzed, a numbness which spread from his feet to his head, accompanied by chills and growing heat for some minutes. He was hoarse and felt a pain in the back of his neck.

**On Oct. 12, 1977 at 11:30 p.m**. Santo Antônio do Tauá – Manoel do Espirito Santo, 20, high school student , resident of Santo Antônio do Tauá (town), was in front of his house with some friends, Júlio, Paulo, Deca and Carlito) when he saw a yellow light moving E/W, slowing in speed and stopping about 20 meters from the group.

He said he could see two crew members inside who appeared to be human, one man and a woman; the "man" was on the left side and the woman on the right side of the "apparatus"; both wore glasses (different shape) and communication gear (earphones)...the one on the left (?)... more attentively to the group of people. At the same time the other, behind a horizontal tube (?) ...directed a ray of red light toward the group; having been hit directly, it felt like an electric shock, from the feet to the head; then felt paralyzed (arms and legs immobilized) and semi-conscious. The object gradually began to move away, gaining altitude and speed.

Manoel was able to move again, feeling numb for some minutes.

**DESCRIPTION OF OBJECT**: From a distance it seemed like a reddish-yellow star; it turned more yellow as it came closer. He observed a bluish light in the front top part. It had the shape of a barrel with a thin tube (reddish)... and another, more slender, horizontal (45 degrees) one which emitted the ray of blue light.

The apparent size was 1.20 to 1.40 meters and gave the appearance of being transparent (in the bluish part) with a division between the two crew members. The movement: It climbed straight up in a wavy motion (like a leaf in the wind) until it reached a certain altitude, abruptly varying its speed....

**On Oct. 16, 1977 at 7:30 p.m.** Colares – Wellaide Cecim Carvalho, 24, doctor and head of the Colares Hospital.

Dr. Wellaide affirmed having observed on the days and hours respectively sighted a bright metallic object spinning over the front part of the village (beach of Cajueiro NE at low altitude, 100 meters) at an estimated distance of 1,500 meters without producing the least sound.

She described the objects this way: Conical-cylindrical shape (upper part narrower) having an apparent size at that distance of 3 meters in width and 2 in diameter. It moved in an irregular manner (vertical position on its longitudinal axis), accentuated wavy or rocking motion, all the time making swift stops and turning at the same time.

She says she observed closely, being on one occasion accompanied by other people in front of the local state hospital. She was interviewed by elements of Equipe (team); others affirmed what she said. Staking her ethical and professional reputation, she... made a more complete communication with reference to people who said they had been attacked by rays of light from unknown source (four cases were attended).

She said, besides "crise nervosa," her patients had other symptoms... (Partial paralysis of the body) evidencing a different ... clinical picture when having a crise nervosa where the areas of attack were the extremities.

Her patients reported headaches, debility, dizziness, generalized tremors... and, more importantly, first-degree burns marked by tiny perforations. According to the sex, the males on the neck (jugular) and the women on the chest (only one case). I asked for her personal opinion (why these things were happening), she said she believes the things that have been occurring in the region....

**Oct. 18, 1977 at 11 p.m.** Colares –Claudomira Rodrigues da Paixão, 35 interrogated by the chief of the Second Section Sgt. Flávio.

She said she was sleeping in a hammock in a room with her cousin and her children. She saw a light (the town's electricity had been shut off at 22:00) that traveled all over her body (like a lantern), striking her on the left side of her chest, sucking (blood from it),

The light went down the back of her right hand where it felt as if she had been pricked by needle. She tried to cry out for help but couldn't make a sound. Her body was half-paralyzed.

Everything was totally lit by a greenish light. She felt a strange torpor. She was aroused by her cousin, who also saw the light and screamed. Claudomira cried out, "I am ruined (sic), the 'animal' sucked me.'

She felt great heat in the breast and the back of the right hand, a headache, and pressure on her chest. She was treated by Dr. Wellaide, who sent her to the IML (Instituto Medico Legal, or medical examiner's office in Belém). There she was examined by a doctor and told to come back for another examination.

**Nov. 2, 1977 between 7:00 and 11:30 p.m**. at Rio Guajará-

Olaria Keuffer observed a light moving below tree-top level, lighting up the area like daylight. Because of its brightness the witness couldn't see the structural details. It was circular with a reddish dome on top… giving the impression it was transparent; at a distance of 70 meters it appeared to be about three meters in diameter and two meters high (base to top of dome).

In the bottom a porthole opened and a humanoid-shaped being got out, short but muscular, wearing a tight, dark seamless uniform (light was behind him); it was floating; a reddish beam of light came out of his hand and went straight toward the witness, who ran away.

As the witness was running, he saw the being examine his fishing net. Then the humanoid returned to the object, which then moved toward the witness at low altitude with a searchlight seeking the witness.

The witness ran away across the mud flats and later arrived at a place where his friends were waiting in a boat. As he was telling them about the incident, the object appeared again with a different color, reddish on top and blue green below.

They all fled the place. The humanoid came out again, inspected the boat and then returned to the object, which disappeared beyond the trees. The witness was examined by doctors and psychologists, but no abnormalities were found.

Similar Burns Occurred in Venezuela

To my amazement, while researching this UFO flap in Colares in 1977, I found a letter from the U. S. Ambassador to Venezuela that described exactly the same kind of searing light burning members of a family in a letter published in the *Scientific American* 92 years earlier in 1886.

Here it is:

**Curious Phenomenon in Venezuela**

*To the Editor of the Scientific American:*

The following brief account of a recent strange meteorological occurrence may be of interest to your readers as an addition to the list of electrical eccentricities:

During the night of the 24th of October last, which was rainy and tempestuous, a family of nine persons, sleeping in a hut a few leagues from Maracaibo, were awakened by a loud humming noise and a vivid, dazzling light, which brilliantly illuminated the interior of the house.

The occupants completely terror stricken, and believing, as they relate, that the end of the world had come, threw themselves on their knees and commenced to pray, but their devotions were almost immediately interrupted by violent vomiting, and extensive swellings commenced to appear in the upper part of their bodies, this being particularly noticeable about the face and lips.

It is to be noted that the brilliant lights were not accompanied by a sensation of heat, although there was a smoky appearance and a peculiar smell.

The next morning, the swellings had subsided, leaving upon the face and body large black blotches. No special pain was felt until the ninth day, when the skin peeled off, and these blotches were transformed into virulent raw sores.

The hair of the head fell off upon the side which happened to be underneath when the phenomenon occurred, the same side of the body being, in all nine cases, the more seriously injured.

The remarkable part of the occurrence is that the house was uninjured, all doors and windows being closed at the time.

No trace of lightning could afterward by observed in any part of the building, and all the sufferers unite in saying that there was no detonation, but only the loud humming already mentioned.

Another curious attendant circumstance is that the trees around the house showed no signs of injury until the ninth day, when they suddenly withered, almost simultaneously with the development of the sores upon the bodies of the occupants of the house.

This is perhaps a mere coincidence, but it is remarkable that the same susceptibility to electrical effects, with the same lapse of time, should be observed in both animal and vegetable organisms. I have visited the sufferers, who are now in one of the hospitals of this city; and although their appearance is truly horrible, yet it is hoped that in no case will the injuries prove fatal.

Warner Cowgill. U. S. Consulate, Maracaibo, Venezuela November 17, 1886

## Conclusion on Colares Island

According to ufologists who covered this historic invasion of this island and the harassment of its population, it ceased just as suddenly as it started.

They also agree that the documents released by the Brazilian Air Force were just the tip of the iceberg and that there are probably many more astounding photos and information about this incident the public may never know.

However, some things about this extraordinary event are obvious to me.

1. The UFOs and their occupants had no regard for humans and crudely took their blood and examined their boats and houses like a conquering army.
2. They worked almost exclusively in the dark and hide themselves in the surrounding waterways during the day.
3. They operated with complete impunity and any attempts by Brazilian helicopters to follow them or stop them were feeble and futile.
4. They could have been part of a government testing program, using the island's residents as guinea pigs.
5. Or they could have been part of a joint project between aliens and the government.

While this is terrifying in and of itself, it is what we do not know about the motives of these invaders that is most horrifying.

Why were they so interested in collecting blood samples and to what end will they use this information?

Did they choose this isolated island of fisherman because their cries for help against a flap of UFOs were more likely to be ignored or brushed off by the powers that be as the imaginings of an uneducated and superstitious people?

Could this flap have been one of several exploratory excursions on planet Earth to ascertain our capabilities, vulnerabilities and physical makeup to best plan a quick and deadly future invasion?

The answers to these questions are coming in my opinion, but others believe the incidents were just some sort of mass hysteria triggered by some strange lights in the sky.

An eerily similar story of the invasion of strange creatures taking blood from unsuspecting humans surfaced in my research of major newspapers archives.

It was reported by the *New York Times* Dec. 24, 2002.

The *Times* reported that a rumor that the African country of Malawi's government was colluding with "vampires to collect human blood for international aid agencies in exchange for food" had sparked a surge in vigilante violence.

Although the president of this small nation at the time, Bakill Muluzi, blamed the rumors on his political opponents, terrified villagers took the law in their own hands and stoned one man to death they suspected of helping the vampires. They also beat three Roman Catholic priests because they also suspected them of vampirism.

In an attempt to quell the rising violence, Mr. Muluzi assured the people through a hastily called press conference that "no government can go about sucking the blood of its own people," but the rumors would not go away because they were based on the eyewitness accounts of women and children, who claimed they were victims of these strange bloodsuckers.

The Jan. 14, 2003 edition of the *Times* shed more light on the so-called vampires of Malwai by describing them in detail.

### Nefarious Nocturnal Bloodsuckers

"They wear dark clothing, it is said, and carry syringes to draw blood from their drugged victims, who sicken or die," the *Times* reported eyewitnesses saying.

"The creatures have magical powers and a fondness for vanishing in graveyards, but no one has heard of them changing into bats."

Although these modern-day monsters had not been seen drinking blood, in a nation where AIDS is rampant, they were seen carry flashlights and sleeping gas to force themselves on their helpless victims.

**Abandoned Syringes Fuels Vampire Stories**

In a further attempt to counter the growing violent push back from the villagers, the government arrested nearly 40 people. However, the discovery of abandoned syringes fueled even more anger among the villagers, who believed they now had proof they were not delusional.

For example, Elesi Makwinja told the *Times* she narrowly escaped a vampire attack and in fact watched them vanish into thin air. Relatives of a woman in one of the villages also attributed her death to being slowly bled by the vampires.

"We don't know whether they are real people or spirits, but we know they are attacking," said Peter James, the brother of the now deceased woman.

Others believe the villagers were not imagining things.

Charles Kaiya said he remembers a similar vampire scare about 30 years prior to this one. Eventually, the police arrested a man caught with syringes and bottles of blood. Mr. Kaiya added that some theorized the vampires are really government agents drawing the blood of villagers in return for financial aid.

"Maybe it's going to Saudi Arabia to get money," he told the *Times*.

## Chapter 3 – Alien Mutilations

1*UFOs, Black Ops -- or both?*

This brings us to the next type of hostile activity attributed to extraterrestrials: animal mutilations.

This is no joke and even though popular culture makes light of these atrocities, there are no ranchers who have lost many head of livestock who consider it a laughing matter.

As part of my research of this gruesome subject, I scoured the 50 years of newspaper archives and found some bizarre cases that lead me to believe there was much more to these incidents than meets the eye.

## Alien Tool Found at Site of Animal Mutilation

For example, a strange alien tool covered with horse hair that was used to extract the animal's organs was found by a horse's owner Mrs. Burl Lewis when she visited the site of the mutilation for the second time, according to an article in the *Washington Post* published Oct. 10, 1967.

This and other evidence bolstered the claims made by the horse's owners that their animal was attacked and mutilated by extraterrestrials.

An autopsy of the horse named "Snippy," a 3-year-old gelding from a range in Alamosa, Colo., revealed the absence of organs in the abdominal cavity.

**Witnesses to Autopsy**

Four members of the Denver team of National Investigating Committee on Aerial Phenomena (NICAP) witnessed the horse's autopsy by a pathologist, who wished to remain anonymous. They included Dr. and Mrs. Ken Steinnmetz, Dr. Herb Roth and Capt. Dick Cable of the North American Air Dense Command Center in Colorado Springs.

When a pathologist sawed open the horse's brain cavity, he found it empty. Bizarrely, all the flesh had been stripped from the horse's neck and head, leaving only bones.

Ranch owner Mr. Harry King called the owners of the horse when it was discovered dead in a field, and they searched the area together.

To their bewilderment they found areas where the Chico brush had been squashed to within 10 inches of the ground with 15 circular exhaust marks within 100 yards of the horse's carcass. Six similar impressions where found in another area of the ranch.

**Measurements of Impressions**

The investigative committee measured the markings on the ground and found the largest to be a circle 75 feet in diameter. Several smaller circles measured 15 feet in diameter.

As mentioned above, Mrs. Lewis claims to have found an alien instrument used in the horse slaying, and the article reported that when she touched it her hand turned red and began to burn.

A few weeks later, as is so often the case in such reports, a follow-up article was published in a more prominent section of the paper. In the second article, an official state pathologist was quoted as saying the first unnamed pathologist had been mistaken and that the horse had been attacked by a wild animal. There was no mention of the alien device found at the scene of the mutilation, nor were the owners of the horse quoted.

**The truth about cattle mutilations based on FBI documents and expert witnesses**

This is just one case of an animal mutilation, there are scores more documented by many Western rancher.

A 32-page declassified FBI report obtained by me, documents the Bureau's reluctance to investigate a spate of similar cattle mutilations and possible witness intimidation in Colorado despite multiple requested from the late Democratic Sen. Floyd Haskell.

**Excerpts from Haskell's Letter to FBI**

In a letter from Haskell dated Aug. 29, 1975 to Special Agent Theodore Rosack, the Senator pleaded for the FBI to get involved.

"For several months my office has been receiving reports of cattle mutilations throughout Colorado and other western states. At least 130 cases in Colorado alone have been reported to local officials and the Colorado Bureau of Investigation," writes Haskell.

Ranchers Scared

In the letter, Haskell went on to make his case for FBI involvement, telling the FBI that the mutilations were scaring residents out of their wits.

"The bizarre mutilations are frightening in themselves: In virtually all cases, the left ear, left eye, rectum and sex organ of each animal has been cut away and the blood drained from the carcass, but there is no traces of blood left on the ground and no footprints," Haskell wrote.

**Helicopters and Threats**

The closest Haskell came to identify those perpetrating the cattle mutilations occurred when he wrote that "a helicopter was used by those who mutilated the carcasses of the cattle, and several persons have reported being chased by a similar helicopter."

Some UFO researchers, of which I am one, speculate that either (1) the cattle mutilations are part of some elaborate top secret Defense Dept. project, (2) the helicopters where there to catch up with the real extraterrestrial perpetrators, (3) they were assisting the extraterrestrials in their work, or (4) they were trying to dispose of the evidence of the mutilations.

**Internal FBI Memo Speaks of Threats**

In the report, there is also an internal FBI memo mentioning that Dan Edwards, the editor of a local newspaper where the mutilations were taking place, called Haskell stating that he had information "U.S. Army helicopters had been seen in the vicinity "of where some of the cattle were mutilated and that he, Edwards , had been threatened. However, in his letter to the FBI Haskell said he "did not know what sort of threats Edwards had received or by whom."

**FBI No Go**

Despite numerous pleas from a U.S. Senator and reams of evidence about the cattle mutilations that some locals feared would escalate into "human mutilations," then FBI Director Clarence Kelley turned down the written and telephone requests for an FBI investigation in a Sept. 13, 1973 letter to Haskell.

"The information set forth in your letter regarding the mutilation of cattle in Colorado and several other Western states and the reported use of an unidentified helicopter by those individuals responsible has been carefully reviewed," Kelley wrote.

"I regret to inform you that these actions do not constitute a violation of Federal law coming within the FBI's investigative jurisdiction."

Kelley then simple kissed off Haskell and the Colorado ranchers with a bureaucratic good luck, even though they appeared to have provided the Bureau with ample evidence that the organized mutilations were being conducted across state lines.

"I hope the investigation currently being conducted by local law enforcement agencies regarding this matter will soon be successfully concluded," Kelley wrote.

Haskell even threatened to introduce a resolution in the Senate to force the FBI to get involved, only to be told by the agency that he'd have to pass a law to make it happen. Haskell backed off at this point because he knew this would be an impossible task.

## FBI Documents: U.S. Attorney General Spooked by Cattle Mutilations

The cattle mutilations continued and so did other Western senators demanding for an investigation, FBI documents show.

The grizzly and bizarre cattle mutilations shocked even a hardened prosecutor and former judge Attorney General Griffin Bell under the Carter Administration. When he reviewed a packet of extensive information about cattle mutilations forwarded to him by then New Mexico Sen.

Harrison Schmitt, Bell fired off the following letter back to him:

"I must say that the materials sent me indicate the existence of one of the strangest phenomena in my memory," Bell stated in his letter to Schmitt, who joined a long list of Western senators desperately prodding the FBI to investigate a spate of ongoing cattle mutilations occurring in their states during the 1970s.

## Possible Government Cover Up?

Some of the information the former Apollo Astronaut and scientist Sen. Schmitt gave Bell included an investigative piece written by Ed Sanders *for Oui Magazine's* September 1976 issue.

In the lengthy article, Sanders questioned a myriad of eyewitnesses including a former intelligence officer and offered several possible explanations for the cattle mutilations. They included: a black-ops biological warfare research-and-development program run by a team of rogue scientists, the possibility that the mutilations were being perpetrated by UFOs and extraterrestrials --or that some sort of satanic cult might be responsible.

**No Satisfactory Closure**

Finally, in 1979, the FBI caved in because of public pressure and allocated $44,000 to fund an investigation of the cattle mutilation phenomena.

The investigation concluded that the mutilations were mostly the result of the cattle being preyed upon by their natural predators. However, the FBI was forced to admit that at least some of the cases contained anomalies that could not be explained. Unfortunately, the FBI was unable to identify any individuals or groups responsible for the mutilations, nor has the agency been able to stop cattle mutilations that continue to occur to this day.

# Chapter 4 – UFOs Challenging Planes and Troops

As I underscored in the Capt. Mantell case, hostile aliens appear to be the rule, rather than the exception.

## 1976 Case of UFOs disarming and shutting down Iranian F-4 Phantom jets

There are few UFO cases more documented than the hostile encounter that occurred when two Iranian F-4 Phantom fighter jets were scrambled to challenge a formation of strange UFOs spotted flying over Tehran in the early morning hours of Sept. 19, 1976.

What makes this case so interesting and disturbing is that it shows that these unknown objects could not only outmaneuver the Iranian F-4s, but they also had the ability to shut down their weapons, communications and power systems at will.

Excerpt from National Press Club News Conference

At a Nov. 12, 2007 press conference at the National Press Club in Washington D.C., one of the F-4 pilots General Parviz Jafari recounted his harrowing experience.

Jafari told the group of reporters how he tried to intercept an "object which was flashing with intense red, green, orange and blue lights," and how other objects with different shapes separated from the main one, at different times during his close encounter.

"Whenever they were close to me, my weapons were jammed, and my radio communications were garbled. One of the objects headed toward me. I thought it was a missile. I tried to launch a heat seeking missile to it, but my missile panel went out," Jafari said.

"Another followed me when I was descending on the way back. One of the separated objects landed in an open area radiating a high bright light, in which the sands on the ground were visible. We could hear emergency squash all the way, which was reported by other airliners flying at the time and continued for another couple of days. During my interview at headquarters after the incident, an American colonel took notes. When I asked if he thought this was an alien spacecraft, he said he was not quite sure that it was."

## Boeing 747 Trailed by Giant UFO Bigger Than 2 Aircraft Carriers

Today, there are many confirmed sightings of huge, football-field size UFOS, but one of the first and most credible sightings happened in 1987.

It involved the pilot and crew of a JAL flight 1628 on the first leg of a trip from Iceland to Anchorage, Alaska to an ultimate destination of Europe and then Japan. It also documented aggressive action taken by a UFO towards a plane full of human passengers.

In an article published in the *Washington Post* on Jan. 2, 1987, the terrifying story of veteran Boeing 747 cargo jet Capt. Kenju Terauchi and his co-pilot was told.

### Permission for Evasive Acton

The incident occurred on Nov. 17, 1987 when Terauchi radioed the FAA asking for permission to take evasive action against several UFOs that suddenly began to tail him too closely.

"They were flying parallel and then suddenly approached very close," Terauchi told the *Post*. Both FAA and Air Force radar operators confirmed the objects that seemed intent on crashing into the Boeing 747.

Permission was granted and the veteran pilot with 29 years of experience dropped the plane to 4,000 feet after first making a 360-degree turn. However, to the pilot's chagrin, the UFOs followed him without missing a beat.

There were three of them -- two small disc-shaped UFOs and one huge walnut-shaped UFO that was bigger than two aircraft carriers, according to Terauchi.

"It was unbelievable," Terauchi said. The UFOs had followed his plane for 400 miles -- before they suddenly shot off into space.

Although this incident was corroborated by Terauchi, his crew and two radar operators, neither the FAA nor the Air Force conducted a public investigation of the 747's harrowing near collision with a giant UFO. As is so often the case with such events, public officials simply shrug their shoulders and keep mum about the ordeal. I'd love to know what they had to say behind closed doors.

## Pan Am Airline Pilot Tells of Near Collision with UFO

As I research UFOs -- and especially first-hand accounts by airline pilots who have nearly collided with them -- I am always amazed at the hardcore skepticism and mocking such reports elicit.

This is a mindset that I believe has been embedded by a concerted government effort to discredit the whole UFO phenomenon and render it a joke.

The fact is that once a professional pilot takes the extraordinary step of going public, for all intents and purposes, it kills his career. Even if he keeps his job, he is ridiculed and said to be a little "off" when others talk behind his back. It's only when you consider the price such brave individuals pay that you begin to understand why their testimony about UFOs is so credible.

## Strange Air Encounter of Capt. Matthew A. Van Winkle

This is also why when I researched newspaper archives for this report, I took special notice to a first-person account of a Pan Am airliner's near collision with a UFO written by the pilot Capt. Matthew A. Van Winkle and published Mar.12, 1957 in the *Washington Post.*

In the piece, Van Winkle tells of his dangerous encounter with a UFO:

"It looked like it was coming right at me from at most a few hundred yards. As to what 'it' was, I have less an idea today than when I tried to evade it," Van Winkle wrote.

At the time of the aggressive action taken by the UFO, Van Winkle's years of flying experience kicked in as he immediately took evasive action ascending so suddenly that it took 4 minutes to quiet the plane," which had whipped violently on the tail when I pulled her up," he wrote.

"I saw whatever it was slip up under my right wing and knew in an instant it hadn't hit us. Then I had to report to the ground by radio," Van Winkle wrote.

## Fighter Jets Scrambled

The article reports that an "unofficial report" stated that the Strategic Air Command ordered jet fighters scrambled to investigate and pursue the UFO, but soon after the report was sealed and labeled as "classified."

This case mirrors dozens of similar near collisions with aggressive UFOs with aircrafts, but this doesn't seem to make officials publicly curious about such incidents. Instead, those who report them are smeared and ridiculed as we come no closer to finding out what these UFOs really are.

## Soldier Says That He Was Abducted by UFO that Delivers Strange Message

A Chilean soldier and his men say he was abducted by a UFO while on patrol in the Andes foothills and then came back with a substantial time loss – plus a strange message from his extraterrestrial captors.

According to an article published by the *Associated Press* on May 23, 1977, Cpl. Armando Valdes, the patrol leader of a small unit of Chilean soldiers, ordered his men to take up their arms as he went to investigate one of two bright objects that landed only 500 yards away from where he and his men had set up camp for the night in Chile's north desert country.

**Features of the UFO**

According to the soldiers, the UFO shone with a violet light with two points of intense red.

As they watched Valdes, the soldiers claim he simply disappeared. The UFOs soon shot up into the sky and 15 minutes later, Valdes was found lying unconscious at the spot where he had vanished.

Eyewitnesses testified that Valdes regained consciousness about 7 a.m., but that his watch read 4:30 a.m. -- the time of his disappearance. Here's the weird part of this bizarre encounter of the third kind: The soldiers also claim that the date on Corporal Valdes had been advanced five days -- and that he also had about a week's growth of beard!

**Extraterrestrial Message**

According to his men, the first words out of Valdes mouth when he regained consciousness were: "You do not know who we are, or where we come from. But I tell you that we will soon return."

# Chapter 5 – More Government Cover -ups

Still it seems no matter how many times such hostile alien encounters occur, there is never an official acknowledgment publicly that humans might be in trouble

In fact, the opposite is the position is embraced by governments all over the world by discrediting, denying and covering up.

**First Roswell Cover Story Discovered; Blamed Russians for Flying Discs**

The United States kicked off its continuous denial that extraterrestrial or interdimensional visitor were invading our world for more than 70 years,

At the time of the Roswell UFO crash in New Mexico, a cover story blaming the Russians for flying discs had already been successfully floated and added to the FBI Top Secret files.

I recently discovered the article published in the *Milwaukee Sentinel* on July 7, 1947 filed in the FBI's declassified Top-Secret document archives. It tells a convincing story to post

World-War II Americans that blames the Russians for the mysterious and numerous sightings of UFOs that were occurring during this time period. Sound familiar?

It was the perfect cover story for the new phenomena at the time: UFOs.

### Disinformation at Its Best

After a headline which reads: "Russ Tells of 'Atom Saucers,'" an anonymous reporter writes a bizarre story based on information provided by an unnamed source who had supposedly been given this Top Secret information by an unnamed Russian officer from an unnamed Russian tanker that had "recently docked in Los Angeles."

The lead paragraph of this perfect Roswell cover story was sensational and to the point: "Federal agents today investigated a letter to the *Examiner* describing supersonic atom-powered planes resembling the 'flying saucers.'"

The article then goes on to say that these so-called Russian flying saucers are atomic powered and only "8 inches thick, with a kidney-shaped outline and no propellers.

We are then asked to further suspend our disbelief when the article claims that The Russian "pilot lies on his stomach and is artificially cooled against the air friction. The article then goes on to say that the Russian flying saucer is also highly polished. Such a description is obviously tailored to fit a rash of similar descriptions of UFOs being reported by terrified citizens.

But there's more: The cover story even clears up the mystery surrounding UFOs unconventional propulsion.

"Energy is required only for climbing, but no energy is needed for support when the airplane goes along the earth's gravitational contour lines," the article claims.

The unnamed source then explains how this is possible:

"Both upper and lower surfaces are convex, like a giant lens," the source explains. "The lifting force is an entirely different principle found about 10 years ago among unpublished papers of a Russian chemist."

How convenient.

**One of Many Cover Stories**

As I stated before, it is my belief that this is one of the first cover stories fabricated by the United State government and fed to the press to explain away the Roswell UFO crash and a spate of other unexplained UFO sightings occurring in the United States.

Since then, the Roswell incident has morphed into a weather balloon, a Top-Secret balloon surveillance program and a few years ago into a phony UFO piloted by Russian midgets.

The more the Roswell extraterrestrial event is confused and discredited by the U.S. government with a barrage of false cover stories, those in power can keep the truth of what really occurred from the eyes of the masses. Mission accomplished.

Recent declassified video of Navy pilots encountering UFOs near their aircraft carrier, along with a NASA scientist saying life was discovered on Mars back in the 1970's by the first Viking Mars probe, underscores the fact that the U.S. government along with world governments have been hiding the truth about UFOs and life existing on other planetary bodies.

This is certainly nothing new.

## UFOs Crashes Scenes Cordoned Off, Then Covered Up

The origin of the U.S. government's massive and heavy-handed disinformation campaign began in 1947 after the Roswell, New Mexico UFO crash incident.

On Dec. 9, 1965, when a UFO crashed in some woods in Kecksburg, Pa., which is located 30 miles southwest of Pittsburgh, the U.S. government once again cranked up its nefarious, cover-up machine.

According to investigations of the incident competed by the Sci-fi and History channels, soon after residents, volunteer firemen and a radio station reporter reached the scene of the UFO crash, the U.S. Army rushed in, corroded off the area and removed all citizens.

But before the Army came onto the scene, eyewitnesses reported seeing a smoldering, acorn-shaped UFO about the size of a Volkswagen Beetle that had strange hieroglyphics etched around its base.

Since then, debunkers and a NASA report have said that what the eyewitnesses really saw that evening was just the remnants of a Soviet Cosmos 96 satellite that fell from the sky.

**A Soviet Satellite?**

Therefore, the Army cordoned off the area and quickly removed the debris from the area on a flatbed truck, critics of Kecksburg UFO sighting say. Yet this convenient explanation begs the question of whether eyewitnesses including a reporter would have mistaken Russian letters for strange hieroglyphs.

While some might argue both type of symbols is foreign to Americans, others would point out that eyewitnesses described the markings on the base of the UFO as being like Egyptian hieroglyphics – not Russian letters.

Summarily, if it had been only a Russian Cosmos 96 satellite, which is acorn shaped, that crashed into the Kecksburg woods, why did government agents lean so heavily on John Murphy, the reporter and news director of the local radio station WHJB, who witnessed the event?

Before Murphy was about to air a documentary, he complied on the UFO incident, he was visited by two government agents, who met with him for about 30 minutes at the station and later in the evening confiscated some of his audio tapes. In addition, a week after the visit, Murphy complained that all the witnesses he had interviewed called him asking that their interviews not be aired.

Murphy did eventually air the documentary, but it was entirely different than the original, according to some who knew him. After the airing, Murphy reportedly became despondent and refused to talk about the incident again. He left the station and moved to California.

In 1969, Murphy was killed in a hit-and-run accident in California when attempting to cross a street.

Why is that so many UFO investigators meet their demise is such accidents or suicides? Why is it that the governments of the world collectively and sometimes in harmony do everything within their powers to suppress the reality of UFOs and extraterrestrials?

Perhaps there are good reasons. Consider this:

**Uninvited Guests**

For a moment let's pretend what I am about to tell you is reality and not the warped unsubstantiated delusion of some mental patient or crackpot UFO researcher.

And if you have a problem with that — then be a good sport and at least read this like a good fiction tale and suspend your disbelief for just the time it takes you to digest my opening gamut.

**A Shock Wave to Civilization as We Know It**

Near the end of World War II it became apparent to the leadership of the United States, Britain and the then Soviet Union that their pilots were being observed, engaged and even in a few cases attacked by strange crafts capable of flying thousands of miles per hour, then stopping on a dime and maneuvering like a beam of light.

Unfortunately, in recent encounters these so-called "Foo Fighters" are also capable of totally incapacitating our weapons and disappearing from our radar and our sight in a twinkling of an eye.

## Grim Starling Reality

Whether it was mankind's introduction of atomic weaponry to the theater of war, or whether the time just suited these visitors from parts unknown to show themselves, they systematically demonstrated to us they could destroy our planes at will, and could just disarm us if they chose to.

Once the gravity of this situation began to sink into the heads of world leaders like England's Prime Minister Winston Churchill and U.S. President Dwight Eisenhower, they vigorously debated about how they would, or would not, break this grim and startling news to their already war-weary people.

According to recently declassified documents from UK's Department of Defence, Churchill convinced Eisenhower that to disclose such information would destroy the very foundations of our countries and world's civilizations, including its religions and social order.

He and others pointed to the madness, panic and suicides that occurred during and after a young radio producer named Orson Welles when he conducted a mock invasion from Mars in his 8 p.m. radio broadcast on Oct. 30, 1938. The show based on H.G. Wells "War of the Worlds" turned the streets of New Jersey and other places into mayhem as people tuned into the fictional depiction of an outer space invasion in the middle of the program – not realizing that it was just a dramatization.

The world leaders reasoned, and probably correctly, that if the common man suddenly became aware that (1) we are not alone and (2) this technologically superior invaders of our air space were not necessarily friendly – then the top could blow off of civilization as we know it like a manhole pushed high into the sky by an underground explosion.

Thus, both men and their governments decided they would go to any lengths necessary to keep this starling news a secret — more secret than any secret had ever been kept before.

As a former news reporter and student of human nature, I honestly cannot disagree with their decision to do so. It could be that by keeping the wraps on this development they gave us enough time to build some sort of counter strategy to defend ourselves from these uninvited visitors. It also gave the populace enough time to digest the idea that there are "others" after being inundated with carefully crafted science fiction media and an occasional mild UFO incident that government censors hand pick to release for public consumption.

## Is This Why NASA Rejected President Carter's Request for UFO Investigation?

While most people remember that Democratic President Jimmy Carter witnessed a UFO when he was governor of Georgia, few remember his request for an investigation of UFOs being rejected by NASA when he took over the White House.

The *Washington Post* on Dec. 28, 1977 reported that NASA blatantly turned down Carter's request for a probe into UFOs simply saying that such a study would be "wasteful and probably unproductive."

**Unusual Action**

The rejection letter to Carter's request came from NASA's Administrator at the time Robert Frosch to the President's then top science adviser Dr. Frank Press.

**Carter and UFOs**

In 1973, then Gov. Carter said he had seen a UFO in the form of a "glowing light" in the night sky.

"I don't laugh at people anymore when they say they have seen UFOs because I've seen one myself," Carter was quoted in saying.

However, after leaving the presidency when asked about his UFO experience, Carter has blown reporters off and minimized the event -- as being no big deal.

I often wonder why? Perhaps Carter knows much more about UFOs today than he did before and finds it wise not to talk about the subject.

Government Investigators: 'Something Big' Happened at Roswell

In a long-forgotten column published in the *Washington Post*, co-written by the late and controversial investigative columnist Jack Anderson, an unnamed government investigator is quoted as saying "something big" happened at Roswell in July of 1947 and that the Air Force was pulling out all of the stops to keep it covered up.

The Jun. 1, 1995 column Anderson quoted unnamed investigators at the nonpartisan General Accounting Office (GAO) who were trying to obtain Air Force documents about the flying disc crash that had initially been reported to have occurred in Roswell, N.M., but was subsequently classified as only a weather balloon.

The GAO was conducting the special investigation as a result of a request from late New Mexico congressman Rep. Steve Schiff, who had been stonewalled by the Air Force for years in his attempt to once and for all get to the bottom of what really happened in Roswell shortly after World War II.

**Air Force Less Than Open**

According to Anderson, some of the investigators he talked to on background believed the Air Force was using all its assets to keep them off the track of what really occurred at Roswell.

"We do believe that something did happen at Roswell," one source told Anderson. "Something big. We don't know if it was a plane that crashed with a nuclear device on it ...or if it was some other experimental situation. But everything we've seen so far points to an attempt on the part of the Air Force to lead anybody that looks at this down another track."

While the GAO never publicly stated their investigators' hunches in the finished investigative report, the agency did chide the Air Force for destroying all the documents regarding Roswell without proper authorization.

Therefore, the investigation came up empty handed.

**Scientists Rejected Air Force's Conclusion UFOs Were 'Interplanetary Spaceships'**

The former chief of the Air Force's first Top Secret investigation of UFOs "Project Blue Book" says that a panel of scientists rejected even top military brass' conclusion that flying saucers were in fact interplanetary spaceships, according to a long forgotten article written by the *Associated Press*.

In the article that was published Jan. 19, 1956, during a time when a wave of UFO sightings occurred, Former Air Force Capt. Edward J. Ruppelt told a reporter the following earth-changing news:

"A panel of scientists in January 1953, rejected an unofficial Air Force analysis, prepared by a staff headed by Maj. Dewey Fournet, that UFOs were interplanetary spaceships." Ruppelt said.

He added that the spaceship conclusion was supported by some officers "at command levels just a notch below" Maj. Gen. John A. Samford, at that time Air Force Director of intelligence.

## Early Admission by Navy Commander That UFOs Were Alien Spaceships

The more research I do in credible newspapers' archives from the early era of UFO sightings, the more evidence I find confirming at an early stage of the game that flying discs were in fact viewed by United States military leaders as outer-worldly space craft.

This was apparently before the intelligence community clamped down hard on such comments and before it had its Psychological Operations machine put a massive domestic disinformation campaign in place.

**Candid Remarks by Naval Officer**

For example, an article published in the Feb. 23, 1950 edition of the *Washington Post* quotes a Comdr. Robert B. McLaughlin, a Naval Academy graduate and guided-missile expert, as saying he was convinced that "flying saucers were spaceships piloted by strangers from other planets."

McLaughlin then was quoted as saying that he knew of an incident where two UFOs had outrun a Navy rocket.

In the article, which was not followed up, the Commander said in April of 1949 a balloon launched from the missile testing grounds in White Sands Proving Grounds in New Mexico was able to track one of the mysterious flying saucers.

"Computations showed the saucer was discus-shaped, 105 feet in diameter, flying at the altitude of 56 miles at a speed of five miles per second," the commander said.

## Chapter 6 – Even More Troubling Cases
**Spate of Silent Giant UFOs Spotted Over Iowa**

In more recent decades, a spate of credible eyewitnesses has been constantly reporting silent, low-flying, football-field size unidentified flying vehicles topped breaking UFO news in 2011.

The sighting of such strange UFOS is nothing new, but the number of sightings has piqued the interest of even UFO skeptics.

I have read the testimony of many eyewitnesses to such events where suddenly a huge triangular object silently floated over their heads at a low altitude.

Many of the witnesses report an eerie silence, while some report an initial sound that gets their attention just before the strange stillness.

One described the stillness as like being enveloped in a vacuum.

**Rash of Sightings in Iowa**

According to the Mutual UFO Network (MUFON), there has been an unusual spike in giant UFO sightings in Iowa.

In fact, here is an excerpt from one such case that occurred on U.S. Highway 30 just West of Ames, Iowa at 3:29 a.m. on Sept. 9, 2011 courtesy of MUFON as reported and written by Beverly Trout.

"As the [anonymous] witness drove eastbound, a sound she describes as a 'whump-rumble' prompted her to look up through her windshield. When she did, she saw a black object hovering over the eastbound lanes of the highway.

The witness estimates the object she saw was 160 to 200 feet ahead of her vehicle, with one end extending beyond the highway's south boundary. Because the witness couldn't see the entire object, she doesn't know how far it extended beyond the highway. The witnesses' estimate of the object's size allows for a calculation that it was traveling at an altitude between 425 and 1,000 feet. The length of the object is estimated between 400 and 1,100 feet.

The witness reported that the shape of the object's underside reminded her or a hovercraft. In a sketch she drew of the object, it is shown with three arcs each containing a row of rectangular-shaped lights. Each of the rectangles emitted a steady white light. This lighting configuration is a vastly different arrangement than the way most witnesses usually describe UFO lighting."

Final Analysis

The strong aspects of this cases are the credibility of the witness, according to MUFON investigators. For me, its vivid detail and its similarity to other giant UFO sightings that elevates its authenticity. However, who's to say that such crafts are not some super-secret U.S. prototype?

It is a fact that low-flying Stealth B-2 bombers performing low altitude exercises at night have been reported as UFOs.

We will just have to wait and see. If the parade of such giant UFOs continues in 2018, perhaps someone will capture enough physical evidence to solve this ongoing mystery.

UFO Blamed for Killing Farm Animals – Documented Case

Meanwhile, some of the strongest evidence of UFOs and extraterrestrial visitors comes from the archives of small-town newspapers. I spend hours searching them, and it's always worth my time. That's because most farmers and ranchers have few agendas and absolutely nothing to gain but ridicule for reporting hostile alien encounters. One wonders why the cynics of these phenomena don't appear to seek such evidence and study it carefully.

One of the strongest cases of farm animals being killed by an unexpected visit from a UFO occurred Feb. 18, 1953, as reported by the *Tabor City Tribune,* in Tabor City, North Carolina, which published a newspaper from 1946 until 1991.

### Mysterious Hovering Object

It seems that Arthur Marlowe of Route 4 was the second Horry County farmer to report a mysterious hovering object over his farm. Not only that, but just 14 hours later, Marlowe found one of his cows, keeled over dead on the very spot where the UFO was hovering.

The strange incident occurred about 12:30 a.m. Saturday morning when Marlowe was suddenly awoken by barking dogs and braying horses. He got up, looked out of the window and saw such a bright light that he thought for sure his barn was on fire. He quickly dressed himself, grabbed his gun and hurried out the door to find to his great surprise a bright shining light being projected from an unknown object about 70 feet above the ground.

Marlowe said he was able to make out three cylindrical beams of light coming from the object. The light being projected from the UFO was so bright that the farmer said he could have read fine print, despite being at least 100 yards away from it. Although he had his gun with him and started to take a shot three time, something told him this wasn't a good idea. He instead decided he would wait to see if it landed and only then get a few sticks of dynamite from his barn to try and cripple it, until authorities could come.

## No Markings and Little Noise

There were no identifying markings on the UFO, and it made little noise, according to the farmer. He watched the UFO faithfully for 25 minutes when it then started to slowly move away. The next day at 2:30 p.m., Marlowe found one of his cows that had been milked in the morning, stone, cold dead on the spot where the light from the UFO had shone. It still had pieces of rye in its mouth.

Soon after, Marlowe discovered that his neighbor, Leon Hardee, who lived one-half a mile from his farm, also suddenly lost a horse that dropped dead for no apparent reason. Hardee had also witnessed the strange light as did Levi Shelleys and Miss Emmadell Prince, all of whom lived in the area.

Moreover, Mark Garner of Myrtle Beach, co-owner of the *Tabor City Tribune,* stated that he also saw a lighted object pass through the skies the same night at 6:20 p.m. Nonetheless, local authorities in a second article in the very same newspaper tried to discount the story, saying that all the witnesses had just seen a U.S. Navy blimp.

Mr. Marlowe, however, vehemently disagreed with this assessment by saying that after the object slowly pulled away it suddenly burst into a high speed of at least 700 miles per hour.

"I don't know of any blimp that can travel that fast," he added

## Reporter Describes Incredible Sighting of Cigar-Shaped UFO over Italy

While for more than 60 years the mainstream media and government officials have scoffed at reports of UFOs and extraterrestrials, both institutions of the status quo have documented many credible and unexplainable cases.

Such is the case of the "Flying 'Cigar' Stops Silent over Rome," which was reported in the *Washington Post* on Sept. 19, 1954 by INS reporter Michael Chinigo.

In an unusual first-person account, reporter Chinigo tells of a cigar-shaped UFO he observed over the skies of Italy on Sept. 18, which was corroborated for 39 minutes by radar.

## Eyewitness Account of Reporter

"What attracted my attention was the strange sound the object emitted as it passed overhead," Chinigo reported. "The sound was not the usual whine of a jet or the droning of an ordinary plane, but rather it was like approaching thunder, but with a staccato effect, a series of explosions that grew louder as the object got closer."

**Eerie Stillness**

Suddenly the explosions stopped, according to Chinigo. "This was followed by dead silence as the 'thing' stopped or appeared to, at a height of about 5 to 6,000 feet," he continued. "Suddenly it shot upward and left an exhaust trail of milky white smoke. It went straight up into the sky. The air was perfectly still, and the smoke remained in a vertical trail."

## Corroborating Witnesses

In the article, Chinigo says that the observatory at Ciampino initially described the UFO as a flying cigar with a big antenna amidships. The United States Defense Dept. pictured it as a "clipped cone" with a smaller surface on the bottom, or as two semi-circular disks, one bigger than the other, with the bigger one on top.

The report then makes the assertion that the UFO could be some sort of Allied experimental machine, or perhaps a British craft "in view of reports of Britain's progress in new type of aircraft."

To this day, the UFO remains a mystery, but similar cigar shaped UFOS have been reported and witnessed by many over the last 50 years.

Shag Harbor UFO Crash Is Canada's Roswell

But no matter how many credible sightings are cataloged and backed up by creditable evidence, the result is always the same: Witnesses are threatened, discredited and the government where the event occurred denies it was anything out of the ordinary.

On such event occurred the night of Oct. 4, 1967 when officers of the Royal Canadian Mounted Police and six civilians witnessed a UFO 60-feet long moving East at high rate of speed crash into Shag Harbour, Nova Scotia, in a strange case that many ufologists consider Canada's Roswell.

Witnesses said that the UFO made a bright splash on impact and that a single white light appeared on the surface of the water for a short amount of time. The police, with help from local fishermen, quickly launched some boats to search the area of the crash for survivors, but none were found.

Witnesses of the search recalled traveling through thick, glittery and yellow foam in order to reach the UFO, which had apparently sunk underwater. The witnesses reported seeing bubbles coming from underneath the surface but could not find the UFO.

**Police Reports Disappear**

The police notified the Canadian Department of Defence of the incident and military search party was launched -- but claimed to come up empty handed. Meanwhile, unofficial sources contended that United States and the then Soviet Union immediately dispatched subs to the area and aggressively searched for the UFO.

The same sources claim the search went on for several days as the UFO played cat and mouse with the military forces of three countries. Finally, the submerged UFO was rescued by a second unidentified object and both surfaced and quickly took off at a high rate of speed to disappear into the horizon.

Even though the Royal Canadian Mounted Police initiated the search, it claims it has no file or documentation of the event, not unlike the U.S. Air Force's claim that it has no file on the Roswell, N. M. UFO crash that occurred in July of 1947 and is still studied more than 6 decades after the event.

The only official acknowledgement of the Shag Harbor UFO crash is a terse, one-page report issued by the

Canadian Department of Defense that creates more questions than it answers.

## Did A Flying Disc with Inhabitants Crash in The Mojave Desert?

One of the most controversial UFO cases of all times is the purported 1950 flying disc crash with inhabitants in the Mojave Desert as told by the late oil producer Silas M. Newton.

The account, which was included in an article by the granddaddy of all UFO researchers Frank Scully, caught the attention of the FBI and its then Director J. Edgar Hoover. It's important to note that this event occurred not quite three years after the UFO crash in Roswell, N.M.

Although the FBI then, as it does today, claims it was and is not interested in UFOs, declassified documents show otherwise -- especially in this 1950 case.

**FBI Identifies Newton as Scully's Source**

In a document I obtained under the Freedom of Information Act, the FBI identified Newton as the source of information about Mojave Desert UFO incident mentioned in Scully's article, which only identified him as "Mr. I."

Many of the names and other information are redacted from the FBI document, but the gist of it is this:

Oilman Newton had leased some land in the Mojave Desert to a company whose members witnessed a flying disc crash on the property. When they ran to the area where the disc had crashed, they found it intact and found a crew of 18 humanoid creatures who had all died in the crash. Newton added that the occupants were small, averaging only 3-feet tall and that the disc was made of a very hard metal that was indestructible.

The FBI continued to investigate Newton until he died in 1972.

Whether Newton's tale was true of not, we will never know. But it is true that his story caused him a lot of grief and FBI attention for the rest of his life.

## UFO Buzzes Small Plane near Washington D.C.

Before UFO reports became the back end of a bad joke and a guarantee of ridicule, a pilot of a small plane flying near Washington D.C, gave a detailed account of his encounter with a flying disc.

The eyewitness account published in the *Washington Post*, on May 27, 1950 is yet another piece of evidence that proves that some UFOs are real and not illusions, or the planet Venus. In the article, private pilot and Library of Congress employee Bertram A. Trotten reported a near collision with a flying disc, about 40 feet in diameter and 10 feet thick.

Trotten had rented a plane and was flying near the then National Airport at about 5,000 feet when he suddenly spotted a flying disc directly underneath his plane.

"This circular object, which seemed to be of aluminum color and glittering on top, came across my path, about 1,000 feet below. I put my ship into dive to get a closer look at it," Trotten said. "As I leveled off the object, whatever it was, accelerated at a terrific speed, pointed somewhat upward as if to gain more altitude, and disappeared."

"I would say it was going 400 to 500 miles per hour as it disappeared to the east. It left a trail of vapor behind. It was in my sight for about one minute and a half."

Again, Trotten's credibility was high. He was test aircraft inspector in World War II and had been flying for 10 years.

## UFO over New Jersey Described As 'Flying Metal Loaf of Bread'

Here's an interesting UFO sighting that recently occurred in New Jersey, courtesy of the Mutual UFO Network (MUFON). Below is the first-hand testimony of the individual who submitted the report. He is a former U.S. Air Force security Officer.

**The New Jersey Sighting**

"It was about 7 p.m., Aug. 15th, 2011, still daylight, clear sky, and no clouds.

I was driving north bound on Black Horse Pike in Bellmawr, NJ. I pulled up to the light at Wendy's and I noticed what I thought was the front end of an airplane, about 75 to 100 yards in the air, crossing the black horse pike about a mile up ahead, going westbound.

It was very low and big. I thought at first, wow, this plane is low, it's going to crash. But it continued. As it continued to cross it stopped, hovered for a few seconds, and then proceeded again. While looking at it, it didn't seem right... The front was rounded, but square, with no windows, but I noticed 3 or 4 windows on the side at the top, with more holes or exhaust ports on the side.

It had a milky white color on the top half, and a dirty silvery metallic bottom. It was made of some type of metal, almost submarine like. As the back end came across, I was expecting to see a tail or tail wings, but there was no tail, just a little hump on the back end. It did not have any wings or rotor blades, it just drifted across the treetops to the west and then it was gone.

I was kind of taken back for a moment, like wow that was really freaking cool. I looked to the person in the car next me, to see if they saw what I saw. But they turned left and showed no interest. I served in the USAF as a security officer back in the late 90's and I have never seen a craft like this... To me it was a mix between a plane, a helicopter, a sub and a space shuttle rolled into one. The best way to describe its shape is: it looked like a flying metal loaf of bread... Very weird, but cool."

## Project Supervisor Claims UFOs Have Threatened U.S. Missile Defense

Long before commanders of U.S. missile installations came out publicly to describe how their weapons had been shut down by interloping UFOs; a project supervisor on the former Minuteman missile program went public about numerous incidents.

In a Dec. 5, 1973 article published by *The Christian Science Monitor,* Raymond Fowler, a project supervisor on a Minuteman missile project near Boston says he was told about the UFO-caused malfunctions at missile sites in North Dakota and Montana.

**Fowler's Story**

According to Fowler, an Air Force officer who had been in one of the subterranean Launch Control Facilities of the North Dakota Minuteman site on Aug. 25, 1966, told Fowler that UFOs had successfully jammed their communication capabilities and had in effect shut their Minuteman Missiles down.

The unnamed officer then told Fowler that "nothing on Earth" has the capability to do this to U.S. defenses. He added that fighters were scrambled, but they could not catch up with the UFOs that disappeared into the horizon at incredible speeds -- breaking all known laws or aerodynamics.

After the event, Air Force intelligence swamped the base ordering all those who had seen or heard anything to keep quiet.

Of course, the Air Force and the Department of Defense denied that any such events occurred.

**Apollo Flight Engineer Tells of UFO Encounter**

Ever since UFOs were first reported there has been a concerted effort by the U.S. government and major media to explain away their reality and discourage their reporting by discrediting and ridiculing those who come forward with eyewitness accounts of the phenomena.

Yet, despite the negative consequences for reporting UFOs, as I stated earlier, some brave individuals are willing to share publicly what they've witnessed. One such highly credible witness is a former Apollo flight engineer Julian Sandoval of Inglewood, Calf.

## Unearthly Sighting near Albuquerque, New Mexico

According to an article published Jul. 11, 1966 in *The Christian Science Monitor*, while driving a car 18 miles north of Albuquerque, N.M. on June 23, Sandoval sighted an object hovering about 12,000 feet in the air at about 3:45 p.m. that in his own words was "nothing like we have."

Consider this statement is not coming from a witness an untrained eye, but from a flight engineer and pilot who at the time was working with the most sophisticated technology known to man. According to his account, Sandoval observed the object with binoculars for 1-1/2 hours, after pulling his car off the road.

## Description of UFO

Sandoval described the UFO's main body as having a "blunt end" and was "incandescent," like a light bulb. He added that there were four lights, which varied from a brilliant greenish color to a tinge of blue on its tail.

"When it would change position it would glow brighter," Sandoval told a reporter. "Its movement led me to believe it used a type of propulsion. "He estimated the size of the UFO to be about 300 feet "from stem to stern."

Finally, the UFO suddenly zipped out of sight at an incredible speed that, once again, defied known laws of aerodynamics.

Sandoval's mother, who was a passenger in his car, also witnessed the event. As mentioned above, in addition to working as a flight engineer, Sandoval was also was a pilot with 7,000 hours of flying time under his belt.

## Florida Governor and 4 Reporters Sight Strange-Shaped UFO

Former President Jimmy Carter wasn't the only governor to personally witness a UFO. Former Governor of Florida W. Haydon Burns and four newspaper reporters watched helplessly as a UFO shadowed Burns campaign plane.

The incident occurred Apr. 26, 1966, according to an *Associated Press* article describing the unsettling incident experienced by five very credible and objective witnesses. Burns, who was running for reelection at the time, appeared to be worried that any elaboration on the event might hurt him politically. Even so, he didn't deny the sighting.

"I will confirm that I saw the same unidentified flying object" the reporters saw, Burns told a group of curious reporters when he disembarked from his campaign plane.

### Reporter Describes UFO

While the UFO buzzed Gov. Burn's plane, co-pilot Herb Bates asked air traffic controllers if they had picked up the UFO on radar, but they hadn't. Nonetheless, the UFO was clearly described by Jack Ledden, a political reporter:

"In shape it resembled two inverted saucers or parentheses, connected by a long pole," he said. "The light was solid and not like that produced by a string of bulbs."

### Charred Alien Hand Found in Strange Meteorite

A charred alien hand was found in the remains of a meteorite that landed on a farm in Bakersville, Calif., according the late edition of *The Day Book* published on Jun. 2, 1916 in Chicago.

Donned the "flaming hand" by locals, the strange appendage fell from the sky, according to Henry Prantl, the owner of the farm where the object landed.

Prantl told a reporter that the hand "shot from the sky with a great white light."

Local scientists who examined the hand, which appeared like a human hand burned off at the wrist, noted that the thumb and little finger were unusually long and there were even nails remaining on some of the fingers.

At first, they speculated that the object was part of a meteorite, but when they closely examined the object that contained the hand, they found it was unlike any material they had ever seen before. The object was extremely light weigh -- yet incredibly strong.

But such sightings aren't just a phenomenon of the 20$^{th}$ and 21st centuries.

Here is one strange incident I found published in a newspaper article just after the American Civil War.:

Almost 100 years before Roswell, a UFO crashed in a remote wilderness of Missouri, according to an article published in the Missouri Democrat on Oct. 19, 1865, a few months after the American Civil War ended. The story was picked up later by several other newspapers, including the New York, *Brooklyn Daily Eagle.*

The eyewitness to this event was James Lumley, a long-time Rocky Mountain trapper, who said that will trapping in the isolated mountains about 100 miles above the Great Falls of Upper Missouri, he witnessed a curious sight one evening just after sunset.

He said he saw a bright object in the sky that broke into pieces, like a skyrocket. A few minutes later, he heard an explosion that jarred the earth where he was camped. This occurred a few seconds after he heard what sounded like a tornado sweep through the thick woods around him.

### Path of Destruction

Lumley followed the path until he came to the side of a mountain that had what appeared to be a huge stone driven through it.

What Lumley had first thought was stone turned out to be some sort of vehicle, which was divided into various compartments. Lumley was shocked to find what he described as some sort of "hieroglyphics" carved into the surface of its strange shaft, as though by "human hands."

Lumley also found what appeared to be fragments of glass scattered around the remaining piece of the vehicle, which he concluded to a small portion of the whole. Lumley also reported that there was a strange black liquid on the ground.

This is where the newspaper article speculates that the vehicle could have come from another planet in our solar system, while Lumley reasoned the strange vehicle must have been used by some "animated beings."

No follow-up article ever appeared in any publication, and whether Lumley or anyone else ever returned to the crash site is not known.

## Children Describe Small Silky Aliens Exiting UFO

Perhaps one of the most interesting but strange cases of extraterrestrial sightings is that of the close encounter experienced by a brother and sister in the French commune of Cussac.

It was on a sunny morning Aug. 29, 1967 at 8 a.m. when 13-year-old Francois and his 9-year-old sister Anne Marie and their dog Mendor led a group of cows to pasture as part of their daily chores.

While the cows grazed, the two siblings played cards until about 10:30 a.m., when some of the cows decided to cross a low wall that marked the property of a neighbor.

When Francois rose to stop the cows from crossing, he saw something he would never forget as long as he lived.

The boy noticed four small beings behind a hedge across the road where the cows were heading. At first, he thought they were other children. This explains why his sister who also spotted them cried out asking them if they wanted to play.

But as she did, Francois got a sick feeling in his stomach as he got a closer look. The beings were not children at all. They were "silky black" humanoid creatures without any distinctive faces or clothing. Moreover, their sizes ranged from 3 to 4 feet in height, with two of the beings smaller than the others.

Francois also noticed that they all have fine limbs and normal heads, except the craniums and chins appeared more pronounced than humans—plus they seemed to have beards. The creatures had been unaware of the children's presence, but when Anne Marie called out to them, mistaking them for playmates, they immediately dove behind the hedge trying to stay out of sight.

In order to see where the creatures had gone, the children then climbed on top of the wall where they witnessed the strange visitors busily working on a brilliant sphere the size of a small truck. The children reported that the craft sparkled so brightly that it was painful to look at for more than a few seconds.

UFOs have been frequenting the United States' skies for at least 150 years or more.

Here's a photo of one of the earliest known UFO sightings captured in Mt. Washington, New Hampshire in 1870.

During the 1890's there was a great wave of UFO sightings at time before airplanes had even been invented.

Newspaper Account

On the night of April 9, a strange object in the sky was seen by thousands in Chicago.

"The moving object was first observed by Mr. Robert Lowen, of Sherman Avenue. He was standing in the store door when his attention was attracted by a moving light in the heavens. The light appeared to be over the lake, a short way out, and was moving in a westerly direction.

Mr. Lowen took a strong field glass and looked at the object. He was able to discern four lights close together and moving in unison. The first light was a bright white light and appeared to be a searchlight; directly back of this was a smaller green light, and further to the rear were a white and green light close together."

According to the article, the skies over Chicago that evening were "swarming with them."

As they do today, the authorities of the time tried to explain the sightings away by claiming that the people were mistaken and had only observed a bright star or the planet Venus.

### Are UFOs, Mirages and Ghosts Just Images Slipping Through Dimensional Tears?

Recently released accounts of a U.S. Navy's fighter pilot's encounter with a UFO at sea, once again made me think about an old theory I have been kicking around in my head for years.

The pilot's account described a UFO, although moving at high speeds near the water and being able to maneuver at extreme speeds only a few feet above the ocean, he noted that the UFOs did not create any turbulence.

When I read that my mind clicked back to a time when I was a kid driving on a country road one bright summer's day and noticed a body of water in front of me on an otherwise dry, hot road. When I saw it, I was a first puzzled because we had been going through a drought and the entire county was bone dry.

It was then my grandfather explained to me that the water I saw would disappear when we got close to it because it was just a mirage. He was right and I learned that day that nature had quite a few tricks up her sleeve and mirages were one of them. What appeared to be water on the road was just a reflection of water from somewhere else being delivered via a natural atmospheric refraction. It was simply an optical illusion.

So when witnesses of close encounters with UFOs report that these massive crafts often make no noise, or create no turbulence, it makes me wonder if there is indeed a natural phenomenon like mirages that occurs naturally reflecting images light years away, or centuries away from place to place, or time to time: a tear in the fabric of time and space, if you will?

## A Nanosecond Vision of the Other

My own personal experiences with such time or dimensional tears go something like this: I am sitting on my couch in my living room next to my wife and a couple of friends when for a nanosecond I see an unknown figure sitting in a chair across from me. Just as the figure is beginning to take full form, it's gone as fast as it came.

The person or being was as real as you or me, but it faded somewhere in time or space's infinite fabric. Was it past — a little before, or future a little beyond present? Was it an image from a galaxy far away, or even an alternative universe?

That leads me to my next question. Does the time continuum wear thin in places sometimes, or have temporary anomalies or glitches like a computer program or my memory?

## Ghosts in an Historic Mansion

Or how about the time I went to visit a historic mansion and when I entered the room, I smelled roses that weren't there and thought I felt a summer breeze — but it was the dead of winter.

Another time tear or sensual anomaly? There are those who contend that strong emotions or places that sit atop mounts of quartz playback time recordings, time and time again. That's how they explain the ageless phenomenon some call ghosts, or hauntings.

For instance, I have had some strong déjà vu experiences, haven't you? Like the time I was walking in Annapolis and suddenly every old townhouse looked familiar.

For a few nanoseconds, I felt like I was someone else and that someone else was experiencing all the emotions, memories of a special moment — a moment that happened a long time ago — but it was suddenly made present for me. Then who was I at that moment — a moment suspended in a time tear?

Yet, since I have no scientific proof, I am afraid for now, my thoughts are still in the realm of pure conjecture

**Unanswered Questions**

And so, this report ends as it began: raising questions and offering incomplete answers. At this stage of the game, I am not sure I will ever know the whole truth, but bits and pieces are revealed, and they can be summed up for me this way:

- UFOs and the creatures that made them and travel in them are real. There is just too much evidence to refute this fact.
- Where these beings come from or who they are still a mystery.
- What they want from us is still a secret. But it seems they are interested in our bodies and our reproductive organs specifically.
- They will not hesitate to eliminate us, if they believe it is in their best interest.
- We do not know what the world's governments and ruling classes know about them, or what kind of understandings or agreements they may have made with these unknown entities.

In fact, a contingency plan on how to survive if our world was invaded by an intellectually and technologically superior alien invasion force is already in existence, based on declassified documents.

## NSA Secretly Developed Survival Strategies in Case of Extraterrestrial Invasion

While the highest levels of U.S. government denied and continue today to downplay the existence of extraterrestrials and their invasion of our air space and land, it has not stopped at least one of the United States' most secretive agencies to prepare a survival plan in the event of an alien invasion.

In 1968, a declassified draft report from the super-secret National Security Agency outlined a 6-step strategy it says mankind must embrace if we are to survive an extraterrestrial invasion.

In the preface of the little-known, once top secret paper, the unidentified analyst states that it would be dangerous for the United States to *assume that UFOs are not real and that such an attitude could leave us wide open for attack from our earthbound enemies such as the Russians.*

Various scenarios

This chilling draft report explores various UFO scenarios, but it minces no words when it lays out mankind's options for survival if it turns out to that UFOs and extraterrestrials are real — and decide to make their move.

"If 'they' discover you, it is an old but hardly invalid rule of thumb, 'they' are your technological superiors," the report says. "Human history has shown us time and again the tragic results of a confrontation between a technologically superior civilization and a technologically inferior people. The 'inferior' is usually subject to conquest."

6-Step Strategy for Human Survival

The NSA document concedes that if extraterrestrials decide to invade, we are at their mercy. But the paper offers a 6-step strategy for humankind's survival:

1. Full and honest acceptance of the nature of the inferiorities separating you from the advantages of the other people.

2. Compete national solidarity in all positions taken in dealing with the other culture.

3. Highly controlled and limited intercourse with the other side — doing only those actions advantageous to the foreigner which you are absolutely forced to do by circumstances.

4. A correct but friendly attitude toward the other people.

5. A national eagerness to learn everything possible about the other culture — its technological and cultural strengths and weaknesses. This often involves sending selected groups and individuals to the other's country to become one of his kind, or even to help him in his wars against other adversaries.

6. Adopting as many of the advantages of the opposing people as you can and doing it as fast as possible — while still protecting your own identity by molding each new knowledge increment into your own cultural cast.

Could our government already be following this strategy now for the last five decades? This would explain a lot about reports of the military being involved in cattle mutilations. Of course, this is purely speculation on my part.

## Bonus Report – Ancient Astronaut Papers

As a former news reporter, I am used to researching countless government documents in search of a key word, sentence or paragraph that will shed some light on a hot story.

The existence of ancient astronauts, or extraterrestrial visitors who allegedly helped shape our world's civilizations and religions is one such story, especially today when UFOs and so-called alien abductions have morphed into a vibrant new age religion.

So, when I discovered a four-page declassified top-secret FBI document carefully recording every word of an obscure Ufologist giving a talk in a small auditorium in 1960, it caught my attention. This is the same FBI that claimed at the time it had no interest in UFOs and that they were just natural phenomena, man-made aircraft or hoaxes. Upon closely scrutinizing the documents, to my surprise I found that the individual the FBI was spying on was presenting a concise ancient-astronaut theory that included scientific and technological facts that wouldn't be discovered for more than 50 years.

It was then that I decided to share my findings with those like-minded individuals that might find this vintage Ufologist's take on ancient astronauts as interesting as I did. Unlike today's ancient astronaut theorists, this unnamed Ufologist offered concrete motives for the extraterrestrial visitors as well as the governments and institutions that denied their existence at all costs.

This report is concise and to the point, and I've concluded it with another document I recently happened upon in the FBI's vault that is relevant to this report. It is a handwritten note by J. Edgar Hoover himself acknowledging the Bureau's desire to examine the "flying discs" that were in the possession of the U. S. Army. I've included copies of these documents at the end of this report I chose to name "The Ancient Astronaut Papers."

Cordially,

**Chet Dembeck**

# Chapter 1 – The Discovery

When I stumbled upon this unassuming report in the FBI's "vault" of declassified top-secret documents describing the surveilling of an obscure meeting held by a Ufologist more than half a century ago, I wondered why the founding director of the FBI, J. Edgar Hoover, had so much interest in what appeared to be just another group of early flying saucer enthusiasts.

However, when I began to read the detailed account of what the Ufologist, who was being spied on had to say, it piqued my interest. And after a while I began to believe that this lecture to a small group in 1960 was far more significant than it first appeared. After reading the report for the third time, instead of shrugging my shoulders and moving on, I felt a little like somebody who went to a flea market looking for a reproduction of a masterpiece for his living room, only to find an original Rembrandt or a Picasso. That's because I had chanced upon one of the first historically documented expositions of an "ancient astronaut theory" that had been kept out of public view for decades.

Today, such theories abound in the media; they are embraced by some as a new religion. But in 1960 such an intricate description of ancient astronauts and how they changed our world was pretty much nonexistent. The fact is this report shows that years before Erich von Daniken published his controversial, ancient astronaut blockbuster "Chariots of the Gods" in 1967, someone had already researched and was sharing with others the theory that extraterrestrials had indeed visited us, shaped our world and were still continuing to do so.

The meeting of about 250 people was held at Pipps Auditorium located in City Park Denver. The only details about the speaker revealed in the FBI's report were that he had been in the "flying game" for more than 30 years, operated a Civil Aeronautics Authority airfield and spent his spare time recruiting others to his UFO group through public talks that drew small crowds of the curious.

## Answers Many Questions

It's my opinion, this FBI report reveals a most concise, authoritative and logical explanation for the origin of UFOS and extraterrestrials. It also explains the reason for their presence now and throughout recorded history, as well as the surprising motivation behind the U.S. government's virulent disinformation campaign and its iron-fisted policy to keep the reality of UFOs and extraterrestrials a secret.

## Catastrophic Polar Shift

The FBI must have been concerned about the Ufologist's revelations gaining traction because the agent carefully chronicled the demographics of the gathering, "The audience was comprised of a majority of older individuals and also the majority of the audience was female," the agent wrote. "There were few young people, although some family groups." This apparently was good news to Hoover. That's because as history teaches us, no movement can really grow exponentially without the activism of youthful members.

During a presentation that lasted for several hours, the agent wrote that the Ufologist "gave a lecture that was more of a religious-economics lecture than one of unidentified flying objects." This seemed to surprise the agent, but the integration of UFOs, the economy and man's spiritual progress has always been the holistic approach embraced by serious researchers of the subject. But before the Ufologist took the holistic approach in his presentation, the agent reported that the mystery man played a 45-minute movie, which included shots of "things purported to be flying saucers, and then a number of interviews from individuals from all walks of life regarding sightings they had made of such unidentified flying objects."

**Ancient Astronaut Theory**

Once the credibility of the UFO phenomena and witnesses to them was established, the Ufologist then began his in-depth reveal, telling his flock of curious listeners that ancient astronauts had indeed seeded our planet with many kinds of animals in a Noah's Ark scenario, which is a story that has been recorded by just about every civilization that ever existed. He said this restocking event had become necessary because of a cataclysmic polar shift that wiped out the dinosaurs.

In my opinion, this part of the Ufologist's talk gives some credence to many of his claims because it is based in real science. As early as 1872 Charles Etienne Brasseur de Bourbourg, a French scholar and expert in ancient Mexican myths, discovered mention of cataclysmic events in ancient Mesoamerican myths that were sparked by a sudden shifting of the Earth's axis. Furthermore, in 1948, electrical engineer Hugh Auchincloss Brown hypothesized that there had been several catastrophic pole shifts throughout earth's history triggered by excess accumulation of ice at the poles. In 1950, Russian scholar Immanuel Velikovsky theorized in his book "Worlds in Collision" that the planet Venus originated from Jupiter as a comet and during two near approaches created devastating polar shifts. He also based his hypothesis on the accounts in ancient books from various cultures throughout the world. Finally, in 1958 college professor Charles Hapgood wrote a book with a foreword by Albert Einstein called "The Earth's Shifting Crust" in which he also contended that such radical polar shifts occurred about every 20,000 to 30,000 years.

Although the Ufologist didn't go into which polar –shifting theory he embraced, he did say that one of these events had made the earth the perfect environment for a colony of male ancient astronauts, who after arriving on our planet soon grew tired of waiting for their female counterparts to arrive from the stars. Perhaps their journey to the third planet from the Sun had been interrupted. So, they decided to mate with "intelligent, upright walking animals, which was the race of Eve." The intriguing element of this early ancient astronaut scenario is that it backed up in scripture from the Old Testament. In the next chapter, I will share some of my own research which corroborates what the Ufologist revealed that spring night in 1960.

## Chapter 2 – The Watchers

The controversy surrounding the Old Testament "Book of Enoch" will always be with us as more theologies reject this unique chronicle than accept it as part of the cannon of the Bible. This is understandable because when interpreted literally, it makes little sense.

The famous R.H. Charles' translation of the ancient book was first published in 1912. Then in 1948 with the discovery the Dead Sea Scrolls, seven fragmentary copies of the Aramaic text of the book were discovered. In later years, several portions of the Greek text surfaced.

**True Events**

It is my belief that Enoch was writing about true events and real experiences using the language and belief system of his ancient times to describe what he perceived as supernatural spiritual beings at war with one another. In truth, I believe Enoch really was witnessing two groups of ancient astronauts from a civilization millions of years ahead of man technologically, who were fighting over whether such an advanced civilization had the right to interfere, intermarry and conquer a primitive species. In my opinion, it is only when we view the so-called "Watchers" or "angels" as extraterrestrial visitors or ancient astronauts that this prophet's epic account makes any sense.

**Shipwrecked or Observation Post?**

I am going to give you the original scripture first, immediately followed by my interpretation of Enoch's writings.

***CHAPTER VI.***

*1. And it came to pass when the children of men had multiplied that in those days were born unto them beautiful and comely daughters.*

*2. And the angels, the children of the heaven, saw and lusted after them, and said to one another: 'Come, let us choose us wives from among the children of men and beget us children.'*

*3. And Semjâzâ, who was their leader, said unto them: 'I fear ye will not indeed agree to do this deed, and I alone shall have to pay the penalty of a great sin.'*

*4. And they all answered him and said: 'Let us all swear an oath, and all bind ourselves by mutual imprecations not to abandon this plan but to do this thing.'*

*5. Then sware they all together and bound themselves by mutual imprecations upon it.*

*6. And they were in all two hundred; who descended ˜in the days˜ of **Jared** on the summit of Mount Hermon, and they called it Mount Hermon, because they had sworn and bound themselves by mutual imprecations upon it.*

*7. And these are the names of their leaders: Sêmîazâz, their leader, Arâkîba, Râmêêl, Kôkabîêl, Tâmîêl, Râmîêl, Dânêl, Êzêqêêl, Barâqîjâl, Asâêl, Armârôs, Batârêl, Anânêl, Zaqîêl, Samsâpêêl, Satarêl, Tûrêl, Jômjâêl, Sariêl.*

*8. These are their chiefs of tens.*

## CHAPTER VII.

*1. And all the others together with them took unto themselves wives, and each chose for himself one, and they began to go in unto them and to defile themselves with them, and they taught them charms and enchantments, and the cutting of roots, and made them acquainted with plants.*

**My interpretation of chapter six and seven of the Book of Enoch is as follows:**

An expedition of extraterrestrials either crashed or was shipped down to earth to observe mankind and watch its progress -- thus the term "Watchers." This is no different than what some of our embedded scientists do in the unexplored wilds with animals or secluded Amazon tribes. They observe, tag and try to learn as much as they can about their subjects without destroying their culture or interfering with their affairs. Again, I am speaking of today -- and not during the period of past European colonialism.

**Gap in Time**

Whether these visitors had crashed or had been transported to the ancient Middle East is not known. But according to Enoch's account, the 200 of them, who had become residents of the area, started to find earth women quite attractive. My best guess is that a long period of time had passed between when this crew had been dropped off or crashed on earth; therefore, as a group they decided it was time to procreate with the natives because they weren't sure if their mother ship would ever be returning. Or this action could have been purely a matter of survival. Perhaps their women had died, or perhaps they were dwindling in numbers and believed it was necessary to take action to preserve their kind. Or, perhaps they were just horny.

Interestingly, Enoch writes that their leader Semjâzâ openly expressed great concern about such a move; in fact, he told his fellow extraterrestrials that he would be held responsible and pay a heavy price for allowing such sexual copulation with earthlings. At this, his crew assured the leader that they had his back, which appeared to ease Semjâzâ reservations enough to give them the final O.K. -- and even join in. It could also be that he had no other choice and sensed if he tried to stop them his life would be in danger.

## Broke the Prime Directive

It was soon after that the 200 visitors descended Mount Hermon, a place where so-called angels and God often communicated with the prophets, and took themselves human wives, therefore breaking the "prime directive," using a Star Trek term. In the next passage, Enoch begins to outline the consequences of these extraterrestrials mating with local women. Immediately, the visitors began to teach their wives basic chemistry and later they would teach their offspring the advantages of technology as applied to warfare with other humans. Soon after mating with humans, the ancient astronauts had sowed the seeds for the disaster that followed.

Here's how Enoch describes it in chapter 8 and 9, immediately followed by my interpretation.

## *CHAPTER VIII.*

*1. And Azâzêl taught men to make swords, and knives, and shields, and breastplates, and made known to them* **the metals** *~of the earth~ and the art of working them, and bracelets, and ornaments, and the use of antimony, and the beautifying of the eyelids, and all kinds of costly stones, and all colouring tinctures.*

*2. And there arose much godlessness, and they committed fornication, and they were led astray, and became corrupt in all their ways. Semjâzâ taught enchantments, and root-cuttings, Armârôs the resolving of enchantments, Barâqîjâl, [paragraph continues] (taught) astrology, Kôkabêl the constellations,* **Ezêqêêl the knowledge of the clouds**, *~Araqiêl the signs of the earth, Shamsiêl the signs of the sun~, and Sariêl the course of the moon. And as men perished, they cried, and their cry went up to heaven.*

## CHAPTER IX.

*1. And then Michael, Uriel, Raphael, and Gabriel looked down from heaven and saw much blood being shed upon the earth, and all lawlessness being wrought upon the earth.*

*2. And they said one to another: 'The earth made without inhabitant cries the voice of their crying† up to the gates of heaven.*

*3 ˜And now to you, the holy ones of heaven˜, the souls of men make their suit, saying, "Bring our cause before the Most High.".'*

*4. And they said to the Lord of the ages: 'Lord of lords, God of gods, King of kings, ˜and God of the ages˜, the throne of Thy glory (standeth) unto all the generations of the ages, and Thy name holy and glorious and blessed unto all the ages!*

*5. Thou hast made all things, and power over all things hast Thou: and all things are naked and open in Thy sight, and Thou seest all things, and nothing can hide itself from Thee.*

*6. Thou seest what Azâzêl hath done, who hath taught all unrighteousness on earth and revealed the eternal secrets which were (preserved) in heaven, which men were striving to **learn**:*

*7. And Semjâzâ, to whom Thou hast given authority to bear rule over his associates.*

*8. And they have gone to the daughters of men upon the earth, and have slept with the women, and have defiled themselves, and revealed to them all kinds of sins.*

*9. And the women have borne giants, and the whole earth has thereby been filled with blood and unrighteousness.*

*10. And now, behold, the souls of those who have died are crying and making their suit to the gates of heaven, and their lamentations have ascended: and cannot **cease** because of the lawless deeds which are wrought on the earth.*

*11. And Thou knowest all things before they come to pass, and [paragraph continues] Thou seest these things and Thou dost suffer them, and Thou dost not say to us what we are to do to them in regard to these.'*

## My interpretation of chapters eight and nine of the Book of Enoch

In chapter eight Enoch tells of the extraterrestrials not only copulating with earth women -- but also teaching earth men how to forge superior weaponry from metals. This would no doubt change the balance of power between the local clans, tribes and the extraterrestrials. Enoch also reports that the "watchers" corrupted the earthlings' culture by introducing them to jewelry, make up and promiscuous sex.

## New Science and Technologies

But even more harmful was the fact that the extraterrestrials were teaching their earth wives meteorology, medicine and astronomy, which Enoch describes in his primitive terms as "enchantments" and "knowledge of the clouds."

**Hybrid Offspring**

Still, the most grievous act the visitors committed that shook the very foundations of the earth was the fact the ancient astronauts were producing hybrid children, who Enoch describes as giants. Remember, a man who stood more than 6-foot-tall would have been considered a giant in an era when the average man only stood about 5 feet. In addition, Enoch alludes to the fact that the extraterrestrials, their offspring and the earthlings they took under their wings were creating bloody havoc on the rest of the region's tribes and easily conquering them. These primitive tribes were no match for the extraterrestrials and their offspring.

In chapter nine, Enoch tells us that the extraterrestrial superiors of this rogue group of ancient astronauts had become aware of their actions and were not pleased at all. In fact, in future chapters he cites how they plan and take severe action against the rebels. So, you can see that the Ufologist in the FBI's report was not just pulling his claims of ancient astronauts out of the air; he obviously was well read in the intertwining of Earth's cultures and the biblical history of these extraterrestrial beings.

## Chapter 3 – Ancient Astronauts and Religions

This Ufologist then went on to tell his potential followers that Moses and other prophets were given the 10 Commandments and other spiritual and moral revelations directly from extraterrestrials. He also credited ancient astronauts with providing "manna from heaven" to many different groups of people on earth who were facing extinction through starvation. The mysterious Ufologist further stated that references to manna from heaven could be found in Native American stories handed down for generations that told of corn and potatoes – potatoes were not known in Europe at this time – being brought to them by a "flaming canoe." The Ufologist contended that this refers to a spaceship because the Indians considered the canoe their highest form of transportation. He added that cultures throughout the ancient world referred to these same extraterrestrial vehicles as "winged chariots and winged white horses." While such speculation is commonplace today, in 1960 this was a radical concept.

**Ties between Jesus Christ & Ancient Astronauts**

However, some of the concepts the Ufologist put forth that evening long ago, will still raise eyebrows today and spark cries of blasphemy. Here is what he said:

"Jesus was born of Mary, who was a space person sent here already pregnant in order to show the earth people the proper way to live," he said.

My own research has found that claims of a God-incarnate savior being born of a virgin such as Mary are not confined to Christianity. In his book "The World's 16 Crucified Saviors," written in the late 1800s by researcher and spiritualist Kersey Graves, he lists the many claims in various world cultures of divine saviors of mankind being born of a virgin.

"From the religious records of India, Egypt, Persia, Greece, Rome, Mexico, Thibet, etc. Maia, mother of Sakia and Yasoda of Chrishna; Celestine, mother of the crucified Zulis; Chimalman, mother of Quex-alcote; Semele, mother of the Egyptian Bacchus, and Minerva, mother of the Grecian Bacchus; Prudence, mother of Hercules; Alcmene, mother of Alcides; Shing-Mon, mother-of Yu, and Mayence, mother of Hesus, were all as confidently believed to be pure, holy and chaste virgins, while giving birth to these Gods, sons of God, Saviors and sin-atoning Mediators, as was Mary, mother of Jesus, and long before her time."

The Ufologist went on to claim that the ancient astronauts had their hands in all of the revelations of the great religious teachers and their communications with so-called "angels" was really their communication with ancient astronauts trying to show them the way to live in peace and harmony.

Again, there is corroborating evidence to this statement in Graves' book where he lists the prophets or god-incarnate saviors that have appeared throughout the ages claiming to have communicated with God, angels, or have been seen by their followers ascending into heaven. They include:

1. Chrishna of Hindostan.

2. Budha Sakia of India.

3. Salivahana of Bermuda.

4. Zulis, or Zhule, also Osiris and Orus, of Egypt.

5. Odin of the Scandinavians.

6. Crite of Chaldea.

7. Zoroaster and Mithra of Persia.

8. Baal and Taut, "the only Begotten of God," of Phenicia.

9. Indra of Thibet.

10. Bali of Afghanistan.

11. Jao of Nepaul.

12. Wittoba of the Bilingonese.

13. Thammuz of Syria.

14. Atys of Phrygia.

15. Xamolxis of Thrace.

16. Zoar of the Bonzes.

17. Adad of Assyria.

18. Deva Tat, and Sammonocadam of Siam.

19. Alcides of Thebes.

20. Mikado of the Sintoos.

21. Beddru of Japan.

22 Hesus or Eros, and Bremrillah, of the Druids.

23. Thor, son of Odin, of the Gauls.

24. Cadmus of Greece.

25. Hil and Feta of the Mandaites.

26. Gentaut and Quexalcote of Mexico.

27. Universal Monarch of the Sibyls.

28. Ischy of the Island of Formosa.

29. Divine Teacher of Plato.

30. Holy One of Xaca.

31. Fohi and Tien of China.

32. Adonis, son of the virgin Io of Greece.

33. Ixion and Quirinus of Rome.

34. Prometheus of Caucasus.

35. Mohamud, or Mahomet, of Arabia.

**An Extraterrestrial Rapture**

Despite this worldwide and centuries old intervention by ancient astronauts, the Ufologist then went tell his audience that mankind had so-far failed miserably, and that only a few had embraced what the extraterrestrials were trying to teach them. In the FBI agent's report, he summed up the Ufologist's assertion that when mankind was on the brink of destroying the earth's ecology and themselves through rampant pollution and war, extraterrestrials would suddenly appear and evacuate those who were the last generation of their hybrid offspring.

**Declassified FBI Documents Tell of Warm-Blooded Dinosaurs Revealed by Ufologist**

While you might be thinking by this time that much of what the Ufologist proffered was a mixture of conjecture and pseudoscience, there are parts of his talk that were truly unexplainable.

## Warm-Blooded Dinosaurs

In the report, the FBI agent says the Ufologist claimed that prehistoric dinosaurs had been brought to the earth by extraterrestrials that bred them here because the earth's tropical climate at the time was perfect for creatures with 105-degree body temperatures. This statement alone probably made FBI analysts characterize the unidentified UFO lecturer as a crackpot because until 2011 dinosaurs were thought to be cold-blooded animals more akin to lizards than mammals. But in its June 28, 2011 edition, *Scientific Daily* reported that a recent analysis of dinosaur teeth by scientists at the California Institute of Technology found that the body temperature of this specimen to be 100.8 degrees Fahrenheit. – a far cry from that of a cold-blooded creature. In addition, recent research has found that these so-called cold-blooded behemoths displayed the habits of mammals rather than lizards.

## How Did He Know?

So, the question becomes how did a UFO lecturer 52 years ago know or even think about such a contrary notion that dinosaurs were warm-blooded creatures? Was it just a wild guess of a mad man, or advance scientific information given him by extraterrestrials?

## Bending Light and Alien Invisibility

The Ufologist also told his audience that extraterrestrials were able to keep themselves well-hidden because they had perfected a technology that could "bend light" by using a special magnetic field that rendered them invisible. This is quite interesting considering that many scientists of today are pursuing the same technology to create invisibility for military purposes! *Wired* magazine reported Jan. 25, 2012 that a team of researchers had discovered a way to bend light and render a three-dimensional object invisible. "It's an incredible breakthrough, but one that won't turn soldiers into ghostly GIs just yet," the article said. "So far, researchers have figured out how to cloak free-standing objects from high-frequency wavelengths, like the microwave spectrum. They've still got to tackle the challenge of making a 3-D object invisible at optical wavelengths — what the human eye would be able to see."

So, once again this Ufologist from 1960 appeared to have foreknowledge of technology and science yet to be discovered. According to the agent's report, the Ufologist then went on to say that the sudden uptick in UFO sightings and alien visitations experienced in the 1950s and 1960s was a direct result of the extraterrestrials' concern with United States and other countries testing nuclear bombs above and below ground that could possibly "upset the earth's rotation and, as in the instance of the French bomb explosion in North Africa, actually caused earthquakes."

## Chapter 4 – Reasons for Denial

**Visitors in Touch with World Leaders**

The Ufologist asserted that the extraterrestrials, who were in fact the ancient astronauts described throughout earth's myths and religious books, had contacted world leaders, but that these leaders decided not to divulge this communication. The Ufologist further claimed that officials made a calculated decision not to reveal the extraterrestrials' presence, not because they feared it would panic the masses, but for other more practical reasons such as a worldwide economic collapse precipitated by alien technology.

"Due to the number of scientific discoveries already made and that will be made [as a direct result of alien technology] which are labor saving and of almost permanency so that replacements would not be needed." The Ufologist went as far to say that the world economy "would collapse under ideas brought by space people."

## Would Unlimited Free Energy Cause Chaos?

Today, some speculate that extraterrestrial technology would open the door to free and unlimited energy that could be made available with very little effort worldwide. One only must think about how this would crush the energy industry and all its horizontal and vertical markets to understand how such a development would be feared and shunned by world governments and the international corporations that support them.

One only has to look at the 20$^{th}$ century genius inventor Nikola Tesla, who died nearly penniless in 1943 to see the corporate world's resistance to such a reality. During his lifetime Tesla, who invented the wireless radio and scores of other inventions, claimed to have experienced blinding flashes of light after which revolutionary engineering ideas were planted in his mind. One of those ideas was free energy that could be distributed throughout the world wirelessly. Fear of his free-energy vision motivated Westinghouse to offer Tesla a billion dollars to curtail his research. Tesla ripped up the contact, according to published accounts, but was soon ostracized by corporate America.

So, it is understandable that our present corporate-run world governments would do everything in their power to avoid revealing the reality of extraterrestrials or their superior technology. To do so would shake the very foundations of the world's political and religious institutions. The status quo would be swept away in the twinkling of an eye. A new paradigm would mushroom that could not be controlled by government or religious leaders." Oh, the horror, the horror," would be the chant of the world's oligarchs.

**Declassified Handwritten Hoover Note Confirms Existence of Captured UFOs**

In summary, this is what I have deciphered out of this FBI report I call the "Ancient Astronaut Papers." You may find something altogether different. But before we finish on this topic, I want to share with you another FBI document I recently discovered in its vault.

It is a handwritten note in which former Director of the FBI, J. Edgar Hoover, confirms the existence of recovered flying discs.

The note was a response by Hoover's right-hand man and close lifelong friend Clyde Tolson to a July 10, 1947 request by Army Brigadier General George F. Schulgen requesting FBI help "...in locating and questioning individuals who first sighted the so-called flying discs..." This request came just days after the Roswell, New Mexico UFO crash, or crashes, depending upon which declassified documents you wish to believe. But it is Hoover's response that nails down the fact that he and other leaders of the U.S. intelligence community not only knew of crashed UFOs but were very interested in examining them.

## The Memo

Responding to the General's request for FBI help Tolson wrote on the memo on July 15, "I think we should do this. "Hoover then responded in his own handwriting, "I would do this but before agreeing to it we must insist upon full access to discs recovered. For instance, in the La. case the Army grabbed it and would not let us have it for cursory examination."

## More Controversy

To me, Hoover's note appears to be very cut and dry. Hoover agreed to help the Army on the condition that it allowed the FBI full access to the crashed flying discs, which it didn't in the past. However, as it is with all UFO research, Hoover's unclear handwriting about which disc he is referring to in the note has sparked controversy. Some researchers interpret his initials differently and believe Hoover was referring to a hoax UFO case that occurred around the same time, while others believe he was referring to the Roswell crash.

However, it is my opinion that the No. 1 man in the FBI would have cared little about examining hoax flying saucers, and in fact, was talking about the Roswell crash or crashes in which the Army whisked all the evidence away before Hoover or anyone from the FBI could examine them. The fact is that Hoover and all the intelligence community were interested -- and are still interested in -- ancient astronauts and flying discs. The FBI documents prove it.

As is sometimes the case, if you have any trouble reading these decades years old documents on your handheld device, you can access all the source FBI documents, which is report is based by simply going to http://vault.fbi.gov/

## Appendix – FBI Documents

### 4-page FBI Report on Ufologist's Ancient Astronaut Theories Dated April 26, 1960:

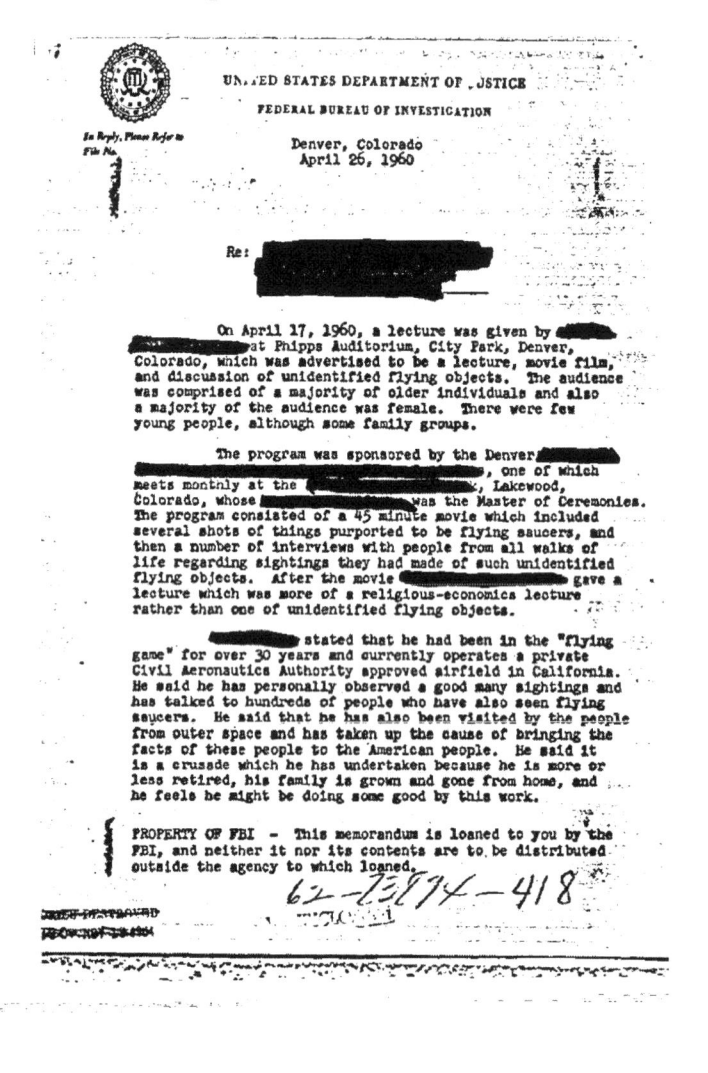

```
UNITED STATES DEPARTMENT OF JUSTICE
FEDERAL BUREAU OF INVESTIGATION

                    Denver, Colorado
                    April 26, 1960

Re: █████████████████████

       On April 17, 1960, a lecture was given by ████
████ at Phipps Auditorium, City Park, Denver,
Colorado, which was advertised to be a lecture, movie film,
and discussion of unidentified flying objects. The audience
was comprised of a majority of older individuals and also
a majority of the audience was female. There were few
young people, although some family groups.

       The program was sponsored by the Denver ████
████████████████████████████, one of which
meets monthly at the ████████████, Lakewood,
Colorado, whose ████████████ was the Master of Ceremonies.
The program consisted of a 45 minute movie which included
several shots of things purported to be flying saucers, and
then a number of interviews with people from all walks of
life regarding sightings they had made of such unidentified
flying objects. After the movie ████████████ gave a
lecture which was more of a religious-economics lecture
rather than one of unidentified flying objects.

       ████████████ stated that he had been in the "flying
game" for over 30 years and currently operates a private
Civil Aeronautics Authority approved airfield in California.
He said he has personally observed a good many sightings and
has talked to hundreds of people who have also seen flying
saucers. He said that he has also been visited by the people
from outer space and has taken up the cause of bringing the
facts of these people to the American people. He said it
is a crusade which he has undertaken because he is more or
less retired, his family is grown and gone from home, and
he feels he might be doing some good by this work.

       PROPERTY OF FBI - This memorandum is loaned to you by the
       FBI, and neither it nor its contents are to be distributed
       outside the agency to which loaned.
                                    62-78874-418
```

RE: ▮▮▮▮▮▮▮▮▮▮

The major part of his lecture was devoted to explaining the occurrences in the Bible as they related to the space people. He said that the only mention of God in the Bible is in the beginning when the universe was being made. He said that after that all references are to "out of the sky" or "out of heaven." He said that this is due to the fact that man, space people, was made by God and that in the beginning of the world the space people came to the earth and left animals here. These were the prehistoric animals which existed at a body temperature of 105 degrees; however, a polar tilt occurred whereby the poles shifted and the tropical climates became covered with ice and vice versa. He said that then the space people again put animals on the earth and this is depicted in the Bible as Noah's Ark. He said that after the polar tilt the temperature to sustain life was 98.6 degrees, which was suitable for space people, so they established a colony and left only males here, intending to bring females at a later date on supply ships. This is reflected in ADAM's not having a wife. He said that ADAM was not an individual but a race of men. He said that this race then intermarried with "intelligent, upright walking animals," which race was EVE. Then when the space people came back in the supply ships they saw what had happened and did not land but ever since due to the origin of ADAM, they have watched over the people on earth. He said that this is recorded in the Bible many times, such as MOSES receiving the Ten Commandments. He said the Ten Commandments are the laws of the space people and men on earth only give them lip service. Also, the manna from heaven was bread supplied by the space people. He also stated that this can be seen from the native stories such as the Indians in America saying that corn and potatoes, unknown in Europe, were brought here by a "flaming canoe." He said this refers to a space ship and the Indians' highest form of transportation was the canoe, so they likened it unto that. He said this can be shown also by the old stories of Winged Chariots and Winged White Horses, which came from out of the sky. He said that JESUS was born of MARY, who was a space person sent here already pregnant in order to show the earth people the proper way to live. He said the space people have watched over us through the years and have tried to help us. He said they have sent their agents to the earth and they appear just as we do; however,

- 2 -

RE: ▓▓▓▓▓▓▓▓▓▓▓▓

they have the power to know your thoughts just as JESUS did. He said this is their means of communication and many of the space people are mute, but they train a certain number of them to speak earth languages.

He said that the space people here on earth are equipped with a "crystal battery" which generates a magnetic field about them which bends light waves so that they, the space people, appear invisible. He said this has resulted in ghost stories such as footsteps, doors opening, and other such phenomena.

He stated that the space people are now gravely concerned with our atom bombs. He said that the explosions of these bombs have upset the earth's rotation and, as in the instance of the French bomb explosion in North Africa, have actually caused earthquakes. He said that the officials on earth are aware of this and this was the reason for the recent Geophysical Year in order to try to determine just what can be done. He said these explosions are forcing the earth toward another polar tilt, which will endanger all mankind. He said that the space people are prepared to evacuate those earth people who have abided by the "Golden Rule" when the polar tilt occurs, but will leave the rest to perish.

He advised that the space people have contacted the officials on earth and have advised them of their concern but this has not been made public. He also said that the radioactive fallout has become extremely dangerous and officials are worried but each power is so greedy of their own power they will not agree to make peace.

▓▓▓▓▓▓▓ also spent some time saying that the U. S. Air Force, who are responsible for investigations on unidentified flying objects, has suppressed information; and as they are responsible only to the Administration, not to the public, as elected officials are, they can get away with this. He said that also the Air Force is afraid that they will be outmoded and disbanded if such information gets out.

He said that the Administration's main concern in not making public any information is that the economy will be

- 3 -

RE: ████████

ruined, not because of any fear that would be engendered in the public. He said this is due to the number of scientific discoveries already made and that will be made which are labor saving and of almost permanency so that replacements would not be needed.

In summation, ████ speech was on these subjects:

(1) Space people related to occurrences in Bible.

(2) Atom Bomb detrimental to earth and universe.

(3) Economy is poor and would collapse under ideas brought by space people.

Throughout his lecture, ████ mentioned only the U. S. economy and Government and the U. S. Air Force. He did refer to the human race numerous times but all references to Government and economy could only be taken as meaning the U. S. One question put to him was whether sightings had been made in Russia or China. He answered this by saying sightings had been reported all over the world, but then specifically mentioned only the U. S., Australia, New Zealand, and New Guinea.

He also mentioned that he was not advocating or asking for any action on the part of the audience because he said evil has a way of destroying itself. He did say that he felt that the audience, of about 250 persons, were the only intelligent people in Denver and he knew they had not come out of curiosity but because they wanted to do the right thing. He said that they were above the average in intelligence and when the critical time came, the world would need people such as this to think and guide.

An application blank was distributed at the meeting for membership in the Denver society of this organization.

- 4 -

## J. Edgar Hoover's Note on Flying Discs Dated July 15, 1947

(Clyde Tolson)

I think we should do this
7-15

(J. Edgar Hoover)

I would do it but before agreeing to it we must insist upon full access to discs recovered. For instance in the Ia. case the Army grabbed it & would not let us have it for cursory examination.

H.

Printed in Poland
by Amazon Fulfillment
Poland Sp. z o.o., Wrocław